Make the Most of Your Time

Discover how to make the most of your time with this unique guide to time perception and manipulation. You'll learn step-by-step instructions for a variety of time-altering techniques. Once you have mastered these techniques, you can use them for creative problem-solving, health and healing, and increased energy and awareness. Learn astral projection, bilocation, distance healing, and remote viewing.

Conversational and positive, *Perfect Timing* cites sources from modern physicists to Zen masters in its presentation of the art of bending and shaping time.

D0974657

About the Author

Von Braschler (Minnesota) is a former editor and publisher of community newspapers and magazines. A lifelong Theosophist, he has led workshops on energetic healing, meditation, and Kirlian photography. He is a certified massage therapist who specializes in pet massage. He is donating half of all personal profit from the sale of this book to animal charities.

To Write to the Author

If you wish to contact the author or would like more information about this book, please write to the author in care of Llewellyn Worldwide and we will forward your request. Both the author and publisher appreciate hearing from you and learning of your enjoyment of this book and how it has helped you. Llewellyn Worldwide cannot guarantee that every letter written to the author can be answered, but all will be forwarded. Please write to:

Von Braschler
℅ Llewellyn Worldwide
P.O. Box 64383, Dept. 0-7387-0212-9
St. Paul, MN 55164-0383, U.S.A.
Please enclose a self-addressed stamped envelope for reply,
or $1.00 to cover costs. If outside U.S.A., enclose
international postal reply coupon.

Many of Llewellyn's authors have websites with additional information and resources. For more information, please visit our website at:

www.llewellyn.com

Mastering Time Perception
for Personal Excellence

PERFECT TIMING

Von Braschler

2002
Llewellyn Publications
St. Paul, Minnesota 55164-0383, U.S.A.

FIRST EDITION
First Printing, 2002

Book design by Michael Maupin
Cover art © 2002 Digital Stock—Digital Concepts
Cover design by Lisa Novak
Interior illustrations by Lauren Foster-MacLeod

Library of Congress Cataloging-in-Publication Data
Braschler, Von, 1947–
    Perfect timing : mastering time perception for personal excellence / Von
    Braschler.—1st ed.
      p. cm.
    Includes bibliographical references and index.
    ISBN 0-7387-0212-9
      1. Time perception. I. Title.

BF468 .B73 2002
153.7'53—dc21   2002019107

Llewellyn Publications
A Division of Llewellyn Worldwide, Ltd.
P.O. Box 64383, Dept. 0-7387-0212-9
St. Paul, MN 55164-0383, U.S.A.
www.llewellyn.com

Printed in the United States of America

Dedicated to my son, James
Thanks for your encouragement

Forthcoming

Conversations with the Dream Mentor

Contents

Introduction

EVERYONE WOULD LIKE to enjoy perfect timing and even time manipulation. But is it possible? If we examine top athletes and Zen masters who live in the moment broadly, we see examples of people who have mastered the metaphysics of time manipulation. Often it leads to performance excellence. Sometimes it means a personal sense of mastery over time and space, with the ability to cross time barriers or "stretch" time whenever desired. Always it involves a change in personal perception and a broadening of who we are and how we fit in the scheme of things. If this sounds like the sort of real magic you want in your life, read on.

Have you ever stared at a pot of water on the stove and wondered with impatience why it seemed to take so long to boil? Did it occur to you at any time that it was simply a matter of your perception of the moment? Have you ever stared at a clock and wondered why time seemed to drag as you watched it? If so, you have the potential of time perception mastery within you.

Let's take a moment to look at the mystery of time and the metaphysics of perceptive awareness. Most people probably believe that time is fixed and measured the same for everyone. Most people outside the study of metaphysics and Eastern mystery schools also probably believe that perceptive awareness is just keeping pace with how people around you see things occurring.

Actually, time is totally invented and an arbitrary rule established as a convenient measure of agreement. Only recently did people measure time carefully at all. Our ancient ancestors arose in the morning when they perceived the sun on their faces (or sensed an urgency). They ended their day when they perceived a need for rest, and when it was too dark to stretch the day any longer. Modern people have learned to stretch the day with artificial light. Some people even lose sleep in the false sense that they can stay up all night, whereas our ancestors went to bed at nightfall and arose with the sun. Surprisingly, our ancestors seemed to have more time for in-depth conversation, reading, quiet walks, and hours of intense contemplation. By contrast, modern people with timesaving devices, speedier communication equipment, faster transportation, and daylight-saving time in this age of bright cities that never sleep nonetheless don't seem to have enough time to get to know their neighbors. Everybody seems to be rushing around, as though they feel they have less time. Could this be a difference in time perception?

Before people started "keeping" time, the universe seemed to measure the passing of events in a different manner. Stars were born, galaxies were formed, and our world took shape over great durations. The Ice Age came and then retreated over an epoch. Great civilizations rose and declined over great ages. Things happened in their own good time. Russian author Helena Blavatsky, in her book *The Secret Doctrine,* described the universe as naturally measuring events of coming and going in a creation cycle as though an exercise of will and intent over long durations, as matter and energy perceive where they want to go and what they want to become. Perception can take a long time, or happen in the twinkling of an eye like a momentous "Aha!" discovery that people sometimes experience very deeply. Change can come slowly or quickly. It depends on how perceptive you are.

Indian sage J. Krishnamurti said that we are living in an age of "a great awakening" of human souls. Most of the world, he said, was sleepwalking through life, not aware of who they are, where they are going, or how they really fit in the grand scheme of things. To finally awaken, in the way Krishnamurti saw as an individual's great challenge, a person would need to experience a momentous "Aha!" deeply with a fundamental paradigm shift in how one sees the self in relation to all of creation and the divine plan. That, too, can happen in the twinkling of an eye, or over a great duration. It all depends on your perceptive awareness. It depends on whether your eyes are really wide open, or if you are sleepwalking through life.

Perceptive awareness, then, is being fully alert and living fully in the moment. It is seeing the trees bend in the wind and the way the birds circle overhead. It is sensing how the trees feel and what problems and joy the birds are experiencing. It is experiencing the full moment around us and not just our little thoughts. It is clearing the mind of future shopping lists and replayed scenes, so you can experience the entirety of the current moment in time. It is putting yourself in the full-frame picture now in front of you in relationship to everything happening around you. It is being fully alive. With that kind of perceptive awareness, a moment can seem to you to last forever. The paradigm shift in your awareness will last a lifetime.

Indian yogis, or *sumadhis,* often claim to have great out-of-body discoveries in which they experience worlds within worlds in what amounts to seconds of real time, if you were to watch them go into deep meditation. These sumadhis are similar somewhat to Native American shamans in how they describe their travel into the world of spirit. There they claim to experience great insights beneficial to their own self-discovery and their tribe's situation. Sometimes they experience these insights with their eyes open, taking into account the hawk descending and the wind blowing through the bent grass. They read the signs all around them, and sort of "tune in." These are not daydreaming flights of fancy. These are moments of superconsciousness in which a person is fully alert.

Being fully alert and aware of everything around them is something that the best ballplayers seem to master. The best ballplayers, after all, are like Native American shamans in the sense that both are impeccable warriors who stand strong and alert in the field around them. How else would you describe the way Michael Jordan could capture the moment and freeze everyone around him with those leaps through the air where he seemed to hang forever? John Jerome's book *The Sweet Spot in Time* describes how the best baseball batters can seemingly slow down time so that fastballs seemed to go in slow motion. How do you make a 100-mile-per-hour fastball seem to slow down so that it just seems to sit there, waiting for you to hit it? Amazingly, some of the best batters in baseball describe an experience where things seem to go in slow motion when they need to take action. How do they do that?

If the mysteries of perfect timing and the mastery of time manipulation really interest you, then turn the page.

CHAPTER 1

Time—an illusion you can control

TIME IS AN illusion. I can demonstrate this with a little story. Actually, it's something that happened to me and my little Triumph sports car—an accident in which I nearly died.

I was returning from an assignment up a mountain road for the newspaper where I worked in Washington State. It was turning dark, so I hurried to get home for something that I was certain could not wait. Because the Triumph always cornered well—even at high speeds—I raced with abandon down a perfectly paved, steep road. As the car roared downhill in fourth gear at around 40 mph, I was unconcerned that the ninety-degree turn that I needed to take at the bottom of the steep hill was fast approaching. Suddenly I noticed that the end of the hill was barricaded with heavy steel guards. It was a drop-off into the deep canyon below.

No problem, I thought. My car could take that sharp turn without even braking. I started to downshift into third gear, but then noticed something at the bottom of the hill where I needed to turn sharply. Rain from the night before had accumulated into a large puddle at the bottom of the hill. I was already entering the puddle, when I was about to shift down. The water started to splash, as the front wheels entered the deep puddle. Then I realized the car was about to hydroplane, skimming in a way that would give me no control over the direction of the car. Not controlling the direction of the car meant that I would crash at high speed into the steel barrier at best, or crash through the barrier and topple over the cliff. It looked grim. And I had only about one second to decide on a defensive measure to prevent an accident.

Here's where the story gets strange. My first thought was to brake—a reflex action. I started to put a foot on the brakes hard, but then stopped. I thought through the consequences of that action and reasoned that I would not be able to stop the hydroplaning car. That was a result of playing back memories of past experiences in hydroplaning cars. (It rains a lot in the Seattle area!) So I put my foot back to the accelerator and considered another approach. Then it hit me: Turn off the key to kill the engine. But that was a stupid idea. I remembered turning off the key to stop an engine once; but that was an entirely different situation from a car racing downhill through a puddle of water straight into a dead-end barrier.

No, I needed to turn the car and fast. Only how? Next I thought about cramping the steering wheel hard to the left and accelerating. Only that would mean that I would hydroplane at an even faster rate into the barrier ahead. How could I turn the car?

At last the answer came to me—the only thing I could think to do in the precious time left. I downshifted at 40 mph all the way down to first gear, then floored the accelerator to make the tires spin as fast as possible, cramping the steering wheel hard left to turn at the last instance.

The result was miraculous! The wildly spinning tires caught just enough of the pavement to spin me around. Only I was a little late. The sports car almost made the ninety-degree turn, but hit a sideways glancing blow against the steel barriers on the passenger's side. Thank goodness I had no passenger along for the ride!

I was so dazed from the accident that I drove slowly down the hill and then aimlessly for quite some time through the back streets and alleys of the town below. Finally, a policeman stopped me. He said that I needed to turn on my lights, as it had become quite dark by now, and he wondered what had happened to my car.

I dropped my head onto the steering wheel, as though coming out of a trance. Then I realized how amazing the whole thing was. How many life-and-death decisions had I made in the course of one second? How many debates and scenarios had I run through my head? Had all of this truly happened in only one second?

The policeman said a witness on the mountain had seen my car "spin around like a top," and glance off the metal barrier. He asked if I hadn't seen what was coming. I muttered something about a puddle of water on the road and asked if I should pay to repair the steel barrier I had struck. He shook his head and just walked away.

I will never believe that one second is a limited amount of time in the way I once did. My one second seemed to last an hour. That's how long it seemed to me. It was all the time I needed; and yet, by normal standards of measurement, it was virtually no time at all; a split second.

You probably have a similar story to tell. Perhaps you were in a life-threatening emergency once, when your whole life passed in front of you. As your precious life hung in the balance, for one split second you took stock of your life, including your loved ones, unfulfilled dreams, and unrealized goals. You considered how motivated you were to fight for your life and more time to live it. In effect, you assessed your whole life and made a momentous decision in a split second. Maybe self-assessment, goal-setting, and decision-making had been tough for you in the past, something you always put off. You just didn't have the time to sort all of this out, you would say. But suddenly, with your life on the line, you processed all of this in a flash. Only you noticed something very strange happening inside of you. Everything seemed to slow down. Things seemed to appear to you in slow motion. You saw your loved ones, and they seemed to pose as though frozen in time. You considered logical arguments and argued them through the steps to completion. All of this takes a long time normally, but for this one instance when you are so sharply focused and alert, you play it all out in one magical moment—a moment that you seemed to control.

Afterward, you gushed to everyone who would listen that the whole thing seemed so strange. You talked on and on about all the things that flashed through your mind in that single second that seemed to last forever, about how time seemed to stand still for you. Nobody else experienced this sort of time shift. Nobody else felt time slow down at that instance. It was purely your personal perception.

Many people who survive fires later describe how they seem to have all the time in the world to review various reactions and routes of escape. Fire spreads very rapidly; people quickly succumb to smoke inhalation. Nonetheless, people in burning buildings often have time to get themselves out and then locate other people and get them out, too. Firemen on the scene sometimes report that family members who are safely out of the fire suddenly disappear in the confusion of the moment to rush through a burning house to drag loved ones to safety.

Of course, acts of heroism often seem to happen in a flash. The hero on the battlefield starts to see things very clearly in slow motion and then takes action that others later report as a surprisingly sudden bolt of daring moves.

How do they do that? It's almost as though they were spirited and dealing suddenly on a nonphysical level of being. Certainly, they see the instance in a different manner than others around them. Yet, they see with great clarity and in great detail. They are focused and attentive.

Hypnosis puts people into a state of focused attention in much the same manner. This is not the so-called hypnosis of the stage magician who tries to trick people into cackling like a chicken or revealing embarrassing secrets. In serious hypnosis, the therapist encourages the subject to enter a state of heightened awareness by quieting his mind of outside noises and inner dialogue. "Clear your mind," she might tell her hypnosis subject. "You are feeling tired. You are going into a deep sleep. You are going deeper, deeper, and deeper . . ."

The hypnotist seeks to put the subject into a state of superconsciousness, entering deep into the subject's subconscious mind. This is outside the influence of the conscious mind where we function socially. This is deeper than skin deep, outside the world of the physical. It is the seat of the soul, where dreams are made.

But there's a trick to entering this magical kingdom, of course. You must will yourself to go there and enter with intent. The hypnotist encourages the subject to allow his body to go "dead" without normal feelings. The hypnotist encourages the subject to become very quiet, still, and focused. Hypnosis subjects allow themselves to enter into a state of superconsciousness by severing their attachment to the physical world. You might say that the subject "wills himself" to enter this state, surrendering control to the subconscious mind. In fact, if hypnosis subjects do not enter this heightened state of consciousness of their own free will, the hypnotist is simply unable to hypnotize them effectively.

You can hypnotize yourself, if you like. Many people practice self-hypnosis to put themselves into a state of heightened awareness. You might consider this as a meditation approach, to put yourself into a state of deep meditation. You might practice self-hypnosis to find out how to deal with a problem. Or perhaps you might hypnotize yourself to see things more clearly, on a much deeper level. As a side benefit, of course, the sleeping body during hypnosis gets a good rest in a very short amount of time. So you can give yourself a quick nap, if you are feeling physically tired, and have deep thoughts at the same time.

It's easy to do. All you need is a straight-back, firm chair and a quiet room. It might be best if you take off your shoes. If you are formally attired, loosen up a little. Pull the tie free, so you can breathe. Sit very erect on the chair, with your feet planted firmly on the ground. Put your hands comfortably on your lap or the top of your thighs, as you are sitting.

Now relax. Begin to clear your mind of all internal chatter and thoughts. Shut off any external noise by tuning it out. Close your eyes and picture a blank, silent screen. Don't proceed until your mind is quieted and uncluttered with thoughts and images that normally just pop in and out throughout the day. Concentrate on stilling the voices and noises that are both external and internal. Start with a quiet, blank screen.

Now concentrate on your hands. They tingle a little when you first focus on them. Then they become heavy and, eventually, they fall asleep.

Concentrate on your legs in the same fashion. Notice how they become heavy, numb, and eventually fall asleep, as you descend deeper and deeper into self-induced hypnosis. Next, concentrate on your face. It becomes heavy, numb, and eventually falls asleep.

Eventually, your whole body is asleep, as you enter the hypnotic state. Notice, however, that your attention is very keen. Free from the weight of body and the confusion of distractions, the higher mind entertains deep thoughts with great clarity. This is pure thought. Notice how agile and quick the thought process becomes in this state. This is the state of heightened awareness or superconsciousness. This is very close to the meditative state of the yogis and great mystics. Thoughts are actually faster in this state of higher consciousness. In fact, thoughts enter from all directions.

This is very different from the conscious mind. The conscious mind is the analytical mind. That might sound better than it is. The conscious mind is sort of like the pocket calculator we use for little day-to-day tasks and sorting things out. It likes simple binary choices, as any computer that you just plug in for quick answers. It tells you "yes" or "no" and "left" or "right." It is part of the physical body or lower ego, as many Hindu mystics see it. It is the part of you that communicates and expresses the personal ego. It talks better than it listens. It's hard-pressed, however, to solve a deeply philosophical question, and it works on real time in the common world of doubt and limitations.

However, the superconsciousness, or higher mind, has no such restrictions. It does not live in the physical world with all of its limitations. Quite literally, your higher mind can ignore the laws of physics, since it's not governed by them. The higher mind does not receive sensory information from the body or physical universe for inspiration. Rather, it reaches out beyond the body and beyond the self. It puts out its antenna to the greater world around the self and listens. This is very different from the conscious mind that is an extension of the individual's personal ego. As an extension of the ego, the conscious mind likes to talk—not listen—making itself known and heard. We all know how good listeners learn better, whereas listening (and learning) is very nearly impossible when you are fully occupied by talking.

The higher mind, by contrast, is a good listener. Once the lower mind surrenders control of it, this higher consciousness sends out its antenna to probe anything it can pick up. Since the higher mind is not a part of the physical self or ego, it is not limited by the laws of the physical universe. It can process an amazing amount of complex, original thought in a very short amount of real time. Because it is a good listener, the higher mind picks up thoughts, ideas, songs, mathematical formulas, pictures, and ideas from the entire universe around you. After all, it is not a closed system, like the conscious mind. It is not limited to what the self knows.

Here's the amazing quality of the higher consciousness with regard to personal time manipulation: Because it is outside of the physical world and its physical laws, it can race at speeds faster than the speed of light, and process an enormous amount of material in the twinkling of an eye. It can take you wherever you want to go and be back almost at the same time you leave.

The true magician or mystic would be quick to point out, however, that you cannot take a meditative journey of discovery without two important qualities. You must exercise your will to take this meditative journey, and you must focus your intent on the journey. Otherwise, it's a bit like meandering off, looking for a grocery store with no sense of direction and no shopping list. You must be fully alert in a heightened sense of awareness and exercise your will and intent to be effective.

The Hindu mystics, who are so good at meditative trances in their eternal quest of self-realization and enlightenment, view much of the lower world, or physical world, as illusion. Compared to the worlds beyond this world, this is not the real world, they might tell you. So much of what we view as certainty and universal truth is simply man-made logic. We are at best only linear thinkers and two-dimensional in our thinking. Yet beyond our physical control is a vast universe of potential other realities.

Many Hindu mystics view time as an illusion, part of a vast, physical world of illusion. They call the confusion that blocks our clear view the veil of *maya,* or illusion. What we seem to see as solid and certain is only real in our physical realm, limited by our internal senses and cultural biases. As Joseph Chilton Pierce pointed out in *The Crack in the Cosmic Egg,* we really do attempt to hold the world together with our joint attention. It is group consensus that defines our world and gives it shape. But if we shift our view from the simple gaze of the crowd to a shaper focus, we begin to see for ourselves with greater objectivity. This means a total shift in consciousness.

This consciousness shift is a personal shift in perspective. It involves a heightened sense of awareness to the full world around you. It means getting outside your physical body where most of us live all day, with a slavish obsession for pampering our base sensations. Life has to be more than feeling comfortable, safe, and pampered. Life has to be more than enjoying creature comforts.

Jesus Christ had much to say about proper pursuits in life. He also said that the kingdom of heaven is within you and that you could be swept up into heaven in the twinkling of an eye. Obviously, he saw this journey as a personal quest and not a group movement.

Krishnamurti also saw this great awakening as a personal discovery. He said that no teacher could show you the way, but that you must be your own student and teacher and find the truth for yourself. Upon making these remarks to a huge international gathering of his faithful followers, Krishnamurti dissolved his worldwide organization and sent his students on their own.

CHAPTER 2

Past, present, and future occur simultaneously

OUR PAST, PRESENT, and future exist simultaneously. I say this with certainty, based on documented journeys of the many mystics who have personally experienced the Akashik records on the astral plane of existence. This is a spirit world beyond our physical realm, as described in many ancient Hindu texts. The proof of this place's existence is that many Indian sages throughout the centuries have personally experienced this ageless oracle where all records are kept and even brought back information previously believed to be unavailable. Hindu belief is that there is no sense of time in the physical sense in this universal hall of records, just as there is no sense of time in the physical sense in the astral world as a whole.

I've experienced the past, present, and future simultaneously myself, in a sense. Like a lot of aging parents, I privately mourned the passing of my child's youth. My son was alive, yet the child was gone. He had simply gotten older. While I loved my older son, I nonetheless mourned the loss of the young toddler I had once known.

Another parent opened my eyes. She said that she had experienced the same sense of loss when her child grew up. I could find the solution to the problem, she told me, in how I perceived my child. The child, she said, is simultaneously the baby, the adolescent, and the adult. In our perceptive reality, we can experience all of these people simultaneously. The energy that was the life essence of the young toddler still burns brightly and cannot be destroyed.

Opening my eyes in this instance was a little like the biblical admonition, "You have eyes, yet you do not see." My physical eyes were open, but my perception was fixated on the past, unable to see beyond it.

Is it really possible that our own past, present, and future can occur simultaneously? Jane Roberts, author of *Seth Speaks* and *Oversoul Seven,* seemed to think so. I know she is right, because I have experienced this myself. Personal experience means a lot to a mystic, because we prefer to experience things firsthand to gather knowledge, rather than read about it secondhand or thirdhand, as in the case of empirical knowledge. The reason is simple. Personal knowledge involves my perceptive awareness and places I have observed in my own moving reality. Other people's experience and perception builds their version of reality, not mine.

My own experience of blurred timelines happened in Oregon, when I was publisher of a local newspaper at the foot of lovely Mt. Hood. The roads there followed the old Barlow Trail Roads of the Oregon pioneers who moved westward in their covered wagons generations ago. I was driving down the mountain on the old Barlow Trail Road one summer just before dusk. I was nearly into town when something strange caught my attention out of the corner of one eye. At the side of the road, I saw an old barn and oddly dressed people filing out of the barn. I slowed down and looked more closely. They were dressed the way we are used to seeing Western pioneers in the early photographs. They were carrying long-handled tools that appeared to be hoes. I felt as though I were watching a movie. They marched into the field with the soft glow of the sinking sun upon them. Then they simply vanished in front of my eyes.

When I got to town, I asked a few older citizens if they'd ever seen anything like that or had heard anything like that before. "Oh, yes," they told me. "Every now and then somebody sees them in that field by the road. And it always seems to happen around dusk or shortly before dusk."

I have talked to other people on Mt. Hood who have seen pioneers sitting beside a broken-down wagon on the road. These ghost images would appear clearly in focus for a moment, and then disappear. They would be seen wearing old costumes and shaggy haircuts and beards. They carried their old rifles and livestock appeared with them. They looked tired, exhausted, and seemingly unaware that anyone was watching them. In a sense, these old-timers are still negotiating the Oregon Trail.

My mother has a similar story about blurred timelines, one she never tires of telling. When she was a girl back on the family farm in North Dakota one summer day, she saw a young man in a white dress shirt who looked out of place. He was walking across the pen in back of the family house toward a gate. He did not seem to notice anyone around him, even though my mother waved at him. She thought she recognized him in a way. He looked like her younger brother, only he appeared to be years older than her brother, who would have been only about ten years old at that time. The man's face was similar, however, and his wavy, black hair looked the same to her, too. He even whistled the same way her brother whistled. But when he opened the gate and walked through it, he just vanished in front of her eyes.

Now this incident didn't make much sense to my mother until she was much older. When she grew up, she could identify the young man without hesitation. That man looked just the way her younger brother looked when he grew up, went to war, and died of tuberculosis shortly after coming home from the navy. His white shirt was the last thing she saw him wear when he visited her on the West Coast. He died shortly after that, never making it back to the old family farm in North Dakota. Or did he? It always seemed to my mother that he chose to go back to the family farm at the time he remembered and loved the best.

Jane Roberts describes time as more or less fluid. People can explore various timelines and various probable realities simultaneously. For example, you might have once dreamed of becoming a ballerina and created a ballerina in your mind. That little ballerina you dreamed of becoming was conceived by you and then energized by your imagination and thought forms. You gave it focused intention and then fed it with your will, willing it to become real. This is real magic.

Later, perhaps, you abandoned this dream of ever becoming a ballerina, deciding that it could never become a physical reality. Nonetheless, you continued to feed the concept with the power of your thoughts and energy on another level, keeping the dream alive. Consequently, your ballerina reality continues to exist in a shadow world of alternate reality.

Followers of the Roberts philosophy, known as Sethians, might even encourage you to look for that ballerina, as she exists in more than your fantasy. This shadow self, after all, was created by the real, constructive force of your thought forms, focused by your intent, and then continually fed by your will, willing it into existence.

Members of Seth International, numbering in the thousands, recognize the probability of alternate realities on a very personal level. They seek out their probable "others" and often celebrate these other probable realities, by wearing appropriate costumes. This is much more than dress-up or role-playing. It is another perception of reality and another perception of timelines. Sethians have discovered on a personal level what Einstein proved on a blackboard: Time is relative.

The relativity of time makes some sense to us on an abstract, intellectual level, but is hard to internalize in our living reality. Because we are linear thinkers, we tend to think of a timeline as starting at one end of a string and then continuing until there is no more string at the other end. We do not assume that the string is ever curled, bent, or shaped in spiral loops. We see everything with a fixed starting point and an end. You might say that we are "dead-end" thinkers, because everything has an end in our minds. But that is just a limitation of our perception. If we could see other probabilities, perhaps new worlds of reality would open up to us!

For many people, it would be miracle enough just to clear the slate and start over again. Many people preoccupy themselves with obsessions about their accumulated debts, sins, or karma. But if you can conceive a new life, you can perceive it.

Krishnamurti grew tired of people always asking the master about the burdens of karma and the possibility of starting a new life through reincarnation. He looked into their faces and knew that the answers were inside of them. They had within them the power to control their destinies, but wanted some sort of magic words. So finally he answered them. Reincarnation, he told them, is an untrue fact. The truth is that you can reincarnate every moment of your life. You are the agents of your own change. If you are perceptive, you can reinvent yourself at will any time you choose.

This is not to say that you can change any other person's reality. Nor can you alter their timeline. They experience life on their own and perceive their own, separate realities. But you can change your own perceptive reality.

Children of the computer age were delighted when they finally got WYSIWYG, or "what-you-see-is-what-you-get" interface. Before that match-up, the screen image didn't always coincide with what they had in front of them or what they were really working on in terms of the computer page. Now this has been fixed on most computers, and WYSIWYG is the norm for modern computer users.

But that doesn't help when you enter the house of distorted mirrors in the carnival funhouse. Here, nothing appears as we believe it to be. But if we look closely, we realize that we are looking at mirrors twisted to distort images of ourselves. We never see ourselves in the mirror, only reflections. In fact, it is very hard to ever see ourselves. What we see is light reflections. Light bounces off objects and back to our eyes as sensors. Our eyes read this light image upside down like an old-fashioned box camera; and then our brain flips the light image right side up for us. It's almost as tricky as the concave and convex mirrors at the carnival, or the carnie who keeps switching the hidden pea from shell to shell in the old pea-shell game of chance. The hand is quicker than the eye, in many cases.

We must distinguish here between seeing in the physical sense and perception in the conceptual sense. We see with our upside-down, light-sensitive eyes. We perceive with our focused attention or awareness. Carlos Castaneda made this distinction quite clear in his books *A Separate Reality* and *Tales of Power*. The sort of "seeing" that Castaneda did as a sorcerer in training was nonphysical on a spirit level. It was heightened attention, much like the Eastern yogis experience in moments of insights into other worlds. It was perceptive awareness.

The young Carlos Castaneda described in detail how he was taught to focus his attention in the physical world as an impeccable warrior aware of everything around him and fully alert in his physical body. Then he was taught by Yaqui shamans to "undo" this ordinary worldview approach and shift his attention to a heightened awareness. In this heightened awareness, he saw more and experienced more than he had ever seen before. This seeing was not physical vision, but perceptive awareness. He learned to accept this new, enlarged reality and responded to it as an active participant.

Henryk Skolimowski in *The Theatre of the Mind* describes the world we perceive as a theatre of the mind where we interact as characters in a play. Only the play is very real to us and, for all practical purposes, as real as real can be. Our perception sets up our reality. You might say that perception creates reality. Skolimowski in his book described the perceptive world we see before us as our moving reality or perceptive reality. Because this is the world we see, we have no choice but to enter it and move within it as a eager performer in a play or motion picture. It's like starring in your own movie. You put everything you have into it—your focused attention, your intent, and your will power.

I met a person once who really does this. He is the psychic Louis Gittner, author of *Listen, Listen, Listen* and *There Is a Rainbow*, among other books. Gittner lives an enchanted life on an enchanted island in the San Juans near Vancouver, British Columbia. His birth and life work were foretold by the "sleeping prophet" Edgar Cayce, for whom Gittner's mother once worked as a secretary. Louis Gittner himself became something of a sleeping prophet on his own in the way Cayce had predicted. He would recline in a dark room and go into a deep, meditative state. Many of his visions in this state are recorded in Brad Steiger's comprehensive biography, *Words from the Source.*

Gittner also receives students who find him hidden away at the Louis Foundation on this remote island. He does not exactly advertise for students, but meets and talks with just about anyone who is able to locate him. He told me that people were drawn mysteriously to his island. He started a roadside inn called the Outlook Inn on the island and became a quiet innkeeper. There he wrote his books and continued his meditative journeys into the world beyond the physical. He would describe his interaction in this nonphysical world to anyone who would ask him, saying that it was pretty simple, really. He would say that anyone could do it, if they really tried. One of his formulas described how to set up perceptive reality and interact in that world. This is his formula:

Conceive, perceive, achieve, and believe.

What a person can perceive and fully conceive, he can achieve—if only he will believe. Our perception sets up our reality. But we must accept it and interact within it. It must become part of our moving reality. We charge it with our energy. Otherwise, it is a stagnant picture, not a moving picture.

Louis Gittner moved in his alternate reality. He described how he would make real efforts to ring a bell set up on a friend's bed, to validate his presence and active performance. This was an out-of-body experience in the sense that the author's physical body was reclining in Gittner's own home, while his nonphysical double was moving about freely. Gittner learned to not only perceive the nonphysical world and listen to its voices, but to interact within it. We can all do that. It requires a shift in your perceptive awareness, focused intent on what you are doing, an exercise of will, and practice.

I can illustrate this for you. Once when I visited Louis Gittner at the Outlook Inn, I asked the psychic author about the "collections of energy" that gathered around him and which spoke through him. He said that I could see them, too, if I wanted. He would tell me where and when to find them.

There were conditions, of course. Gittner told me to sit in a log cabin behind the inn in the evening and watch for them to appear at a certain time. The cabin was actually a rustic chapel that he had constructed with logs brought to the island piece by piece on the state ferry. He held little gatherings there on Sunday mornings. During these meetings, he would reach into people, and discuss things that were heavy on their minds, just by looking into their eyes. It was all pretty magical, I thought.

At night the cabin was dark. There were no electric lights or lanterns. I visited with a friend and my son, James. We considered lighting a candle or something, but decided the darkness must be required. Our instincts proved correct.

According to Gittner, we were waiting for something to appear at midnight. We came half an hour earlier, just in case these appearances were not all that precise according to anybody's watch. We sat on wooden benches, facing to the front of the chapel, where Gittner would stand and address visitors informally on Sunday mornings. We sat quietly and stared into the darkness for any signs of something non-ordinary, not quite certain what this might be and how we would recognize it, should it appear. We waited for what seemed more than an hour. I remember trying to check my watch to see if we had stayed past the appointed time, but couldn't read the watch in the darkness of the log cabin. Finally, we decided that we'd sat on hard benches in the darkness long enough and should leave.

Then they appeared. Everyone saw them. Little flecks of light slipped through the cracks between the logs in the cabin where we had been staring. The tiny lights darted toward the back of the cabin, up the center aisle that divided the benches on either side. The lights reminded me of Tinker Bell, the animated Disney character who was a sort of woodland spirit. What struck me as odd, and made me think that this collection of lights were conscious beings or entities and not just refracted light eking into the cabin, was the direction they flew. They didn't fly in a straight line or entirely together, but sort of swooped into the cabin and then curled their way, more or less in formation, toward the back of the cabin. They didn't pause, but seemed to just disappear when they reached the back of the cabin. I've always concluded that they slipped between the cracks in the logs on the back walls of the building.

We were dumbfounded by what we'd seen—like nothing any of us had ever witnessed before. We sat speechless for a little while and then filed outside. I checked my watch and was able to make out the time. It was about one minute past midnight—the exact time Gittner had said to expect them.

I was filled with regret that I had not tried to communicate with them or engage them in any way, as they passed through the cabin. Indeed, as Gittner explained, they did appear to be collections of energy gathered at that time and place. And they appeared very intelligent and purposeful. They told Gittner about the nature of the universe. All we got out of their appearance was a marvelous light show.

Perhaps the difference was that I had only asked to see them. To assist me and my friends, Gittner told us where and when to see them. Gittner, on the other hand, went deeper into this non-ordinary reality, engaging it in an active and personal way. It became part of his moving reality or theatre of reality, with himself an actor. It took me years to begin to understand how he could do this. I understood how his "conceive-perceive-achieve-believe" formula could allow me to see non-ordinary reality and the unseen world around us. But to enter the world myself as an actor required something else.

I turned to magic. I refer here to the world of natural magic or elemental, practical magic. This approach is as old and time-honored as the midwives and herbalists of the Middle Ages. In fact, it's even older. It dates back to hidden truths of the hermetic order and the mysteries of ancient Egypt.

There are powers latent in people, according to these mystics, if only people can tap them and activate them. I began to think of a pond of water. The water in this pond could be tapped. But it was a stagnant pond. Water, however, could be energized. You could run it through a water wheel or even a hydroelectric dam. The water itself, then, generates energy. So some ponds you tap can be stagnant, while others can be dynamic. It's sort of like Madame Blavatsky's view of the cosmos where everything is constantly in a state of what she called becoming or "be-ness." Matter can become energy, and energy can become matter again. A latent pool of water can become an active pool of energy. In culling the occult secrets of the ages from all around the world, including Zen monasteries, Blavatsky saw a simple, missing ingredient in this transformation process.

True magicians, sorcerers, and shamans learn to focus intent and learn to feed their intent with their will power. Actually, this is not as mysterious as it might seem. Wizards have been doing it for years. Modern psychics continue to do it.

Everything that exists has an intent. Castaneda wrote in his revealing books about Mexican sorcery that true men and women of power became meticulous observers of everything around them in an attempt to understand the underlying intent of things. Even in the mundane world of the physical, we commonly refer to the power of someone who possesses a firm intention. If you are intent on something, you are generally considered to be powerfully motivated and focused on realizing something or transforming something to your own ends. This is just a little taste of true magic.

Your true magic is inside you. It starts with your understanding of the world in its totality. It depends on your ability to generate thought forms, and dispatch them with force. This is personal power; and everyone has some of it. A thought form is something you conjure deep inside you in a proper state of mind. That state of mind must be a collected and focused state. It cannot be dispatched with any clarity or volition. In this sense, it is not random thoughts, scattered thoughts, idle thoughts, or a stream of consciousness. It is a formed and focused thought that is given shape by you, and then dispatched with direction and force at an intended subject as receiver. In short, these are energized thoughts. They have power to reach their marks like an arrow from a crossbow. They have power to shape and move things when launched.

There is a good reason why these personal, focused thought forms can shape and move things. Your will feeds them and transforms them. Just as desire to change energy to matter and matter back to energy acts as the dynamo in Blavatsky's universe, the human will center acts as our personal dynamo of transformation. We feed our thought forms with desire. This desire emanates from the will center located in the region of the human solar plexus. Begin to think of your solar plexus as your will center, the focal point for energizing your thought forms and giving them shape and substance. Think of yourself as a dynamo for change. This is not a big stretch if you consider how the human body is self-regenerative and transforms water, light, air, and food into energy, and repairs itself when broken. Actually, any plant or animal does this. We are all dynamos with transformative abilities.

But intent and will can do nothing for you, if you do not understand the magical quality of perception. If you can conceive of something, it's likely that you can perceive it. Your perception becomes your reality if you believe it. You simply have to learn to trust your eyes—not the physical ones the optometrist keeps tweaking on your measured chart tests, but your inner eyes. The Hindu yogis refer to this as the *third eye* or "psychic eye," located in the sixth chakra of the human body. Everyone has this. Very few people ever exercise it to get it working well.

I want you to try a little exercise. This is something I used to do to practice shifts in personal perceptive awareness. You must employ your inner eye, focused intent, and will power. At the end of this exercise, I believe that you will prove to your own satisfaction that you can indeed control time.

Stopping Time Exercise

For this exercise, you will need:

- A clock
- A quiet, empty room (You don't need distractions. It's just you and the clock. That way, you can more easily focus.)

Directions—Step One

Look intently at the clock and concentrate on making it stop. You will need to get into a meditative state of deep concentration. Try shifting your eyes a little to the left and not looking directly at the clock. This isn't an exercise in good vision but in how much more you can see. Then you will need to formulate this single, powerful thought and give it form. Focus your intent and send the thought form to the clock. Concentrate on your solar plexus and project will power from this will center. Keep the thought pure and keep sending it. Focus your intent. Keep the will power flowing from your mid-section, as though it were the battery to maintain the flow of energy. You must really want to achieve this goal and send will power with great, personal desire. Keep your eye on the second hand and minute hand of the clock, and concentrate all of your personal power on slowing them down.

Step Two

When you sense that the second hand and minute hand have been slowed down, try the second step of this exercise. To validate that you really can control time, focus all of your attention and personal power on making the minute hand of the clock move backward just one minute.

It's important that you do not tense up, but remain focused and positive. Remember, you must change your personal perception. Then you must validate your shifted awareness with belief. Learn to trust your inner eyes. Learn to trust yourself. You hold the world together with your attention. How you focus your attention is your personal decision.

When you sense that the minute hand actually moved backward one minute instead of forward, stop the exercise.

Now consider this. Did you rob the world of one minute? Or, more likely, was it just your world that you altered? It was your moving reality, your perceptive reality. And, yes, the clock did stop and time did move backward just for you. But only for you.

Shamans learned long ago when they wanted to make rain fall on their own little world it was important to confine this to their little spot only. Not everybody wants to get wet at the same time. Nor can you exercise your will over other people's will. They have their own perceptive reality.

Swami Satchidananda once told how his master in India would send him into a quiet room to meditate on putting gasoline into a can with only his thought forms, intent, and will. He created the gasoline, seemingly out of thin air. Later, his master asked him to go into the room and fill a box with money created in the same fashion. Satchidananda realized that he could probably manifest money out of thin air just as easily as he had manifested gasoline for this master. Considering that the money would be counterfeit or taken from someone else more needing, the young Satchidananda left his master and did not return. He had personal power and confidence that he could shape his own reality. But he also had ethics.

CHAPTER 3

How top athletes manipulate time

LIKE A LOT of people, you probably played softball or some other sport as a child, and on one occasion or another experienced the elasticity of time. You noticed that on some occasions everything seemed to go very fast, while other times things seemed to drag on. You may recall waiting in the outfield for what seemed like hours for something to happen. Didn't it seem to you just a little strange how slowly everything seemed to go? Even the pitcher, who threw the ball very fast, seemed to be doing everything in slow motion. The batter would swing very fast at the pitches, but also looked like he was locked into some strange time warp, where every-thing seemed to move slowly.

Can you also remember playing ball when everything seemed to speed up suddenly, and an amazing number of things happened all at once? Perhaps you can recall taking part in a double play when a batter hit the ball and another player snapped it up to toss to another player for an out. Then that player, in turn, tossed it to another player for another out. All of it happened in a couple of seconds.

The best ballplayers, it seems, have learned how to manipulate time whenever it suits them. Perhaps they do this without a great deal of thought or analysis, but they certainly employ all of the key factors of time magicians. They focus their intent, engage their will power, and energize their thought forms. This is personal magic. This is personal power. Everyone can do it. The superstars just do it more easily and more often than the rest of us. We say that they are gifted or superhuman. They are simply focused, intent, and willful.

I'll never forget seeing the upstart Seattle SuperSonics come back against the great Sam Lacey and his Kansas City Kings in the Seattle Coliseum in the early days of the basketball franchise. The young Sonics were down something like 7 points with only about three seconds left on the clock. It looked like an insurmountable lead, with so little time remaining. And this was before the 3-point play, so that every field goal counted only 2 points!

Lenny Wilkins was the player-coach who gathered his group of overachievers in a late-game huddle. He told them not to give up now. He said that three seconds in professional basketball could seem like an eternity, and that anything could happen in that much time if they played smart. Many of the fans started to leave the Coliseum, thinking the game was all but over. A few of us, however, believed in magic.

Apparently, Lenny and his Sonics had the magic, too. They scored a quick basket to cut the lead to 5 points. Then they stole the ball and scored again, bringing the lead down to 3 points. Amazingly, this all had happened in just two seconds! Then they fouled the Kings and got the rebound on the missed free throw by the Kings. They scored again immediately, bringing the lead down to 1 point. Finally they intercepted the inbound pass, and scored again for the victory. If we hadn't seen it with our own eyes, we wouldn't have believed it.

Actually, this happens fairly often in basketball, if you think about it. Many times there will be less than one second left on the game clock. One team is trailing on the scoreboard, but can win the game with last-second heroics. All they have to do is inbound the ball to a player, and have that player shoot the ball into the basket. If you stop to analyze this, it all seems rather miraculous. Yet many teams do inbound the ball, find an open player, and shoot a game-winning basket in less than one second.

The players are all extremely focused, intent on the task at hand, and energized. They see the perfect pass before they make it. They see the ball going through the hoop before they shoot it. They energize their thought forms. They exercise their will power. And they totally believe they can achieve their goal.

It's truly a case of the hand being quicker than the eye. The ball is tossed inbounds before the timekeeper even realizes that play has resumed and he restarts the game clock. The ball leaves the shooter's hand before the buzzer goes off, signifying the end of regulation time.

If you go to almost any basketball game in the world on any given night, you are likely to see something like this. Perhaps it's the end of halftime. Perhaps it's the end of the game. Perhaps it's the end of the quarter. Or perhaps it's the end of overtime. Literally millions of people have witnessed this time manipulation in person or on television. This demonstrates over and over again the elasticity of time. Everybody knows that under normal conditions when heroics are not on the line, a person cannot pass a ball through a crowd to a selected teammate who scores—all in less than one second. Under normal circumstances, most people cannot even locate a person in a crowd in less than one second, let alone pass him a ball.

As the former editor and publisher of a regional sports magazine, I've had great opportunities to observe athletes at critical moments. I covered everything from high-school teams to professional teams, and even covered hardcore recreational sports such as mountain climbing and kayaking. I noticed after a while that the champions in all sports at all levels of competition seem to have one thing in common. All champions learned to seize the moment.

I recall a young swimmer who came out of nowhere at the end of a race to eclipse the field. Her coach told me that she always found a way to win, and would "pick her spot" to "make her move." Still, it seemed uncanny how she could close the big gap between herself and the race leader at the end, when you consider she had to swim nearly twice as fast as she had been swimming throughout the rest of the race. That's a little like the track sprinter who digs down at the end of the race to bolt like a cannon to victory at the end. To the observer, it looks as though they are running against opponents who are moving in slow motion. How can somebody who's been running at top speed suddenly double that speed at the end of a race, when they should be the most tired? It's an obvious display of will power, focused intent, and energized thought power, whereby they conceive of miraculous victory and believe it is possible. And whatever our consciousness can conceive, the body can achieve.

Mountain climbers seize the moment, too. I know it's difficult to think of mountain climbers moving rapidly in the same way a track star might, but it does happen. I have witnessed climbers facing darkness who suddenly move quickly on the mountain to avoid being stranded in a precarious location at night. People who have read about great climbing expeditions will recognize what I'm saying. It doesn't mean that they moved a little faster as descending darkness hurried them along. They moved incredibly fast by any measurement, moving in minutes what otherwise had taken them hours.

My favorite story from my days as a sports photojournalist might be the World Team Tennis event that brought Chris Evert to Seattle to play against the Sea-Port Cascades. This was in 1977, when Evert was at the top of her game. On this evening, however, she was still suffering from stomach flu, and was noticeably ill. She looked weakened and groggy. What we could not see in her was that championship attitude. Evert refused to sit out the matches that were so vital to her team's composite score. She played on sheer determination, it seemed.

The most remarkable example of her focused determination came in the mixed doubles match. The Sea-Port doubles team, led by player-captain Tom Gorman, saw the ailing Chris Evert as the weak link of their opponents across the net. Consequently, they directed as many shots as possible at Evert, particularly point-blank net volleys directly at her body. Now, these sharp net volleys aimed at the body of an opponent are hard for anybody to fend off, let along return successfully. They tend to jam you up, rattle you, and bottle you up. Chris Evert, in particular, was never considered a net player who liked to volley, but generally stayed away from the net in preference to the baseline toward the back of the court. So the strategy of the hometown team to have Tom Gorman batter Evert with balls at the net seemed like a good one.

Evert, however, had a strategy of her own. She stood her ground at the net and returned volley after volley. At times, she looked like a rag doll, as she twisted and squirmed to put a racket in front of her, protecting her body from the abuse as much as returning balls for points. Surprisingly, these jamming body shots at Evert did not produce points for the hometown team. Rather, Evert returned everything they slammed at her.

There is a point in every great athlete's life when she seems to play beyond herself, outside of her body. This is obvious when an athlete is sick at a critical moment. Somehow she seems to get "outside of herself," and pull her sick body along with herself.

Have you ever seen a track star who was too tired or sick to run, and then surprise the crowd by turning in the best performance of the day? That's what we're talking about here. It's my contention that some athletes actually do get outside their bodies. That's something the yogi masters do. They get into a meditative state where they experience a world of unlimited possibilities and timelessness. Many mystics throughout the ages have been known to deprive their bodies of food or sleep or even punish their bodies in attempts to enter a more mystical state in which they get outside the body and enter a nonphysical world of spirit. Sick people, with their attention removed from the mundane world around them, have been known to have mystic experiences of a nonphysical world. There are no physical limitations in a nonphysical world. That is the world they perceive. The world they fully perceive becomes their moving reality.

As a boy, my son was an enthusiastic cyclist, but not a champion athlete. Nonetheless, an incident where James faced a critical moment on a crowded highway one summer day demonstrates the point here. We were bicycling across Vancouver Island, with James in the lead. A drunken driver pulled recklessly onto the highway from a side road and almost struck James from the rear. Unfortunately, James's bike was not equipped with rear-view mirrors to see the car fast approaching him. Nor did my son have time to turn his head around to see the car. There wasn't time. The car was immediately upon him.

I watched with horror; there wasn't even time to scream a warning. What I saw next shocked me. Just as the car was about to strike the bike's back fender, James leapt forward off the bike, much like a frog hopping forward. As he hit the road, the car crumpled the bike behind him. My son rolled to break his fall on the cement highway and then lay flat, so that the car drove over him without hitting him. It was amazing to watch; and I couldn't wait to ask him how he had done it.

His response really puzzled me. He said that something outside of him jumped all of a sudden, pulling him forward. He didn't think about it, measure the distance, or weigh the options. There was no internal discussion, no fear, and no bravado. He said that he was not conscious of the way his body leapfrogged off the front of the bike, rolled, and cleared the car. It was as though another part of him took control and did all of this amazing gymnastics in the split-second of the accident.

Also, he was not hurt whatsoever by the fall or by the car rolling directly over him, with tires on either side of his body. He did not show even a small scratch or bruise. I don't know quite how he did it and could never begin to coach anybody else to duplicate these moves. Yet they were about the only moves he could have made at that moment in time to avoid injury. It is clear that he seized the moment.

Carlos Castaneda discussed seizing the moment with the parable of a cat. He described a cat taken to a veterinary hospital to be euthanized. The cat sensed the immediate danger and jumped out of the owner's arms at exactly the right moment to escape. Castaneda described that as a cat's cubic centimeter of chance. Everybody has a cubic centimeter of chance now and then. The trick, however, is to be alert enough to seize the moment and then have enough personal power to execute the appropriate move at the appropriate instance. Castaneda said that an average person could become a skillful sorcerer and a master of time and space, but first must become what he called an impeccable warrior—toned, fully alert, and fully aware of the physical world.

The greatest athletes are like impeccable warriors. Just look at our battle-clad football players and hockey players. They are the modern warriors. They have toned bodies, are fully alert, and wary of the physical world around them. They see peripherally and nearly behind them. They sense danger and opportunity by surveying the field around them. These warrior athletes—to use author Dan Millman's phrase—possess amazing will power, focused intent, and energized thought forms. They are competitive. They are winners, overcoming great odds. They seize the moment and make it theirs.

How else could you explain basketball great Michael Jordan who could hang in the air during dunk shots for an extra second or two—longer than anyone else could physically manage? With no physical comparison or explanation, we are forced to look beyond physical explanations and consider him a master of time and space—a true magician.

Baseball slugger Mark McGwire set an astounding new record for home runs in one season, obliterating the old mark of Babe Ruth, which stood for many years. One thing that is probably obvious about McGwire whenever fans would look at him is that he is a fine physical specimen with a toned body, alert, and wary of all challenges and opportunities around him. The one thing that is probably not obvious about McGwire when fans watch him is how he is apparently able to slow things down when he's at the plate. To everyone else, the ball would be rocketing toward the plate at approximately 100 mph, almost faster than the eye can see. But to the focused athlete, the ball seems to slow down just for him, and present itself to him. John Jerome's book *The Sweet Spot in Time* describes how many of the best batters have this in common. Somehow, when they need to slow things down to make their big play; they are able to perceive everything happening in slow motion. The ball rolls slowly up to the plate and is easy to see, often appearing larger than life. It's almost as if the ball is waiting for them to hit it. To everyone else, the ball is racing to the plate at a blistering speed, curving, sinking, and breaking in ways that make it almost impossible to track, let alone hit.

It is tempting to call this time manipulation, since the perception of the person who seems to manage this trick is that time has been stretched longer or made shorter. Since this is the perception of the magician, and becomes the way he acts upon the world, it becomes that person's own functional reality. It's really a consciousness shift and an expanded awareness. And, yes, it is real magic, as we will see.

Try this exercise yourself and see if you don't experience a time shift—where a moment in time seems longer to you than you would ordinarily expect.

Sports Experiment

You'll need:
- Baseball
- Baseball bat
- Someone to throw ball to you
- Someone to catch the ball behind you

Step One

This experiment should be done in two phases. In the first phase, the pitcher throws the ball to you for you to hit. These pitches can be

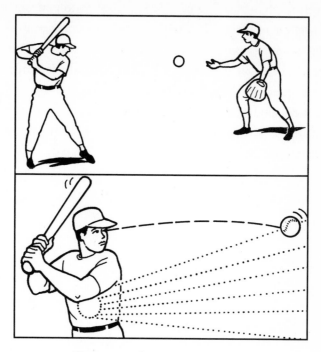

Figure 1 • Sᴘᴏʀᴛs Exᴘᴇʀɪᴍᴇɴᴛ

underhand and slow to avoid injury. It's not important for this experiment that the ball be thrown fast. The critical factor is that the person throwing the ball to you attempts to throw the ball at the same
constant speed each time. (Perhaps your pitcher would like to practice before you begin the experiment to establish a steady speed and
direction for all pitches.) In the first phase, simply clench up on your
bat and attempt to hit the ball.

Step Two

In the second phase, allow yourself to focus consciously on the location and speed of the ball. Clear your mind of all noise and clutter.
Get unnecessary thoughts out of your head. Tune out all sound and
distractions around you. Simply focus on the baseball being pitched
to you. Focus your intent. Imagine hitting it squarely and watching it

sail far through the air. Concentrate on your abdomen and visualize projecting energy from this "will center." You must want to hit the ball and will it to happen. As this next series of pitches come toward you, see the ball big and bold. Fixate on the ball. See only the ball and focus your total intent and will on the ball.

Did the ball appear to be moving slower in the second phase of pitches? If so, you are well on your way to becoming a master of time manipulation.

CHAPTER 4

Being totally conscious in the moment, the "now"

As WE HAVE seen, becoming a master of time and space requires a change in personal perspective. To experience timelessness, you need to focus intently on the moment at hand. You cannot allow your mind to wander over events of the past or wallow in deep concern over the future. You must be in the present moment, fully alert, and clear-headed. In short, you must be totally involved in the "now."

This was the message of teacher and author Alan Watts, who longed for an Eastern teacher to teach Zen meditation to Westerners. Watts considered himself a sort of "advance man," or prophet of a teacher to come. Ironically, Watts himself became that teacher.

Watts taught people in the West how to meditate. He encouraged people to still their internal dialogue and stop the chatter inside their minds. This is a fundamental problem for most of us. Animal behaviorists tell us that we have lost the ability to communicate with other species in our world, because other animals are confused by the seeming contradictions between what we verbalize, our body language, and our thought forms. Indeed, most of us seem at times locked in debate with ourselves with endless internal chatter. We are so preoccupied with our inner thoughts that we are not fully focused on the present situation that confronts us.

Stilling the inner voices might sound easy, but for many it is not. The Buddhists say that the mind must willingly shut itself down before our superconsciousness may engage itself without distraction. In fact, without distraction, our superconsciousness could not engage itself at all. The Buddhists have an expression that the mind is "the slayer of the mind." Moreover, it is the gatekeeper. You might be tempted to think that the mind is the "top cop" in charge of everything. Another way to look at this, however, is that your mind is your jailer. It keeps you confined, in a sort of straightjacket. It's a sort of petty tyrant, claiming to be the big brains—the one in charge. Sadly, it imprisons the higher self, or higher consciousness, which transcends the physical self.

This gate cannot operate half open or half shut. In this sense, it is like a floodgate. Our physical mind jealously guards what it considers to be its rightful territory and role. It wants to be always in charge, because it believes that it is most analytical. But the mind must totally and willingly shut down for our higher consciousness to operate on a higher plane. This is what's required to meditate. Like a lot of people, however, you probably had the idea that you needed to focus on a dot on a wall, or on a certain sound or thought. These are little ways to trick the mind to shut down and allow the higher consciousness to operate. Really, what you need to do is still the mind.

Obviously, this is not easy. The lower mind is a jealous dictator and will not surrender easily. So you must appeal to its reason and allow it to analyze and adjudicate. Once the mind is satisfied that you will be safe and perhaps even rewarded in this proposed encounter, then it should surrender temporary control.

To meditate and enter a state of higher consciousness, however, you also must still the clatter of sound and other distractions around you. Quieting the world around you might seem even more difficult than stilling the inner chatter that runs through your mind. After all, we can hope to have some personal influence over our own bodies, but little influence over the world outside ourselves. Or can we? Remember that the object here is to change our personal perspective. We don't need to stop a bell from clanging to tune it out. We simply need to control our perception. This requires training, practice, and particularly, will power.

In short, we need to stop the world. This is not to say that we can stop the wind, the rain, or a roaring train. We can change our perception of all of this, however. We can tune out the outside sounds. We can tell ourselves not to be distracted by the fragrances around us. We can control our sensory perception.

We do this not to be dead to the beauty and majesty of the physical world around us, but to focus on attaining another higher level of consciousness, without outside distractions. The beauty and aroma of a daffodil can be overpowering. The chatter of children can be either amusing or bothersome, but always hard to ignore. We are not turning our backs on the world around us, but exploring higher consciousness from time to time.

It's almost amusing at times how hard some people work at meditation—even in the East. Krishnamurti told the story of Indian men, serious in their attempts to meditate, who would become angry if children's loud play would disrupt them in their quiet times. The challenge is to tune out the world around us and within us as a prelude to meditation. We can do this very selectively and creatively, in accordance to our needs. We can learn to meditate while simply sitting, walking, or even washing the dishes with proper practice and discipline. In time, you can do it without your eyes shut and hands folded in a quiet, dark room. With practice, you can do it at a moment's notice.

Sometimes this is very useful. Star athletes can sometimes tune out distractions and hear just what they want to hear. They can tune out everything except what they want to see and focus intently on that. That becomes the focal point of their meditation.

If you think about it, you've probably tuned out sounds and slowed down things around you on occasion, too. For example, have you ever been in a crowded, noisy room full of people and tried to shout to somebody in the crowd? They couldn't hear you very well. So then you focused hard on that person and found that you could filter out distracting noises around you to hear what that person was saying. People around you seemed to move in slow motion, as you focused on your friend. That's because you were meditating only on that subject, and only seeing that person's body language and hearing that person's voice. This is selective perception.

I'll never forget the time I first experienced this in a crowded banquet room at a local chamber of commerce gathering. It was an open reception in the little town in Oregon where I was publisher of the community newspaper. The room was crowded with people milling about, elbow to elbow, and extremely noisy. What I heard in walking through the room was a hundred voices at once without focusing on any one, and it was maddening! There was also the rattling of dishes and silverware being set down for a dinner to follow, as the restaurant's wait staff hurriedly set up. On top of this, music filtered into the room from stereo speakers overhead. It was a madhouse.

I was just beginning to wonder how anyone could carry on a conversation with anyone else in that room, when something incredible happened to me. I saw somebody I thought I knew at the opposite end of the room. Suddenly, I honed in on this person. It was like radar tracking. Her back was turned to me. I projected a focused thought at her. She turned around to face me, as though she had heard me. As I walked toward her, we started to talk. We could hear each other perfectly. Somehow we filtered out the other sounds in the room. When we were face to face, we heard only each other. The surrounding room noise had completely disappeared! It was magical, and we both sensed this. It was one of those big "Aha!" moments in life, where you grin ear to ear, your eyes twinkle, and the hair on the back of your head stands on end.

Later, when we finished talking, I walked back across the room. I wondered whether I could make all the voices in the room go away again, all on my own. I concentrated on tuning them out. What happened was almost as amazing as the quiet conversation with my friend. The voices disappeared, and I heard only the music from the stereo speakers! I wondered then whether I could control the volume of the stereo inside my head. That's how I spent the rest of the time in that room—turning the volume of the stereo up and then down in my head. It was astounding how much control I had, when I really tried. I could make the music very quiet, and then very loud, and then very quiet again.

As we sat down to eat, I momentarily shifted my attention to my fellow diners. I concentrated on their hands working the knives and forks on their plates. Suddenly, the sound of silverware scraping against plates became very loud. I heard nothing but the sound of silverware scraping against plates. I did not hear their voices. Then I shifted my attention back to the music, and heard nothing but the music. It was as though I was alone in a quiet room, except for the stereo.

How strange it was! I looked at their mouths moving and heard no sounds coming out of them. Even the people seated next to me made no sounds that I could hear. I became almost frightened that I would never hear the same again, so shifted my attention back to a hearing mode, and heard everyone perfectly. In time, the sound grew deafening again, so I tuned it down just a little.

I realized toward the end of the dinner that I could modulate how much I heard. I could tune in more volume or less volume. It took a certain amount of focused intent to do this. If I let my focused intention loosen even a little, I lost control over what I heard. It felt a little like concentration or attentiveness, but it was more a matter of a shift in my consciousness. I was very aware of something tightening on my spine, beginning at the base of my neck and anchored at the base of my spine. Castaneda used to refer to refer to this shift in conscious awareness as a shift in the assemblage points of the spinal region. All I know is that I seemed to have great control over my hearing.

No one else in the room seemed affected my what I was doing. It was just my own perceptive awareness that I was modulating. But it became very clear to me on that occasion that I was stopping the world.

Castaneda wrote endlessly about stopping the world, a term he may have picked up from Maurice Merleau-Ponty, the early twentieth-century author of *Phenomenology of Perception*. The mystic stops the world by selecting shutting down sensory awareness of the immediate, physical world around him. He does this to leave the ordinary world around him (to use Castaneda's terminology) and enter a non-ordinary reality. The brain no longer processes the physical sensations of smell, touch, hearing, or seeing in the ordinary manner. It is much the same as being asleep and not being conscious of the sounds and smells around you.

This is not to say that being inside your body and fully aware of the beauty and majesty of nature is a bad thing. On the contrary; learning to listen and learn from the sights and sounds of nature around us is very important and advanced training for the shaman to be.

Our immediate exercise here is to learn to enter a meditative state and shift your perceptive awareness away from the ordinary world and ordinary reality. You will need to stop the world. The ordinary world is like a mixing bowl that gets you all caught up inside it. It grinds you up and spits you out in its image. You must learn to control your perceptive awareness if you want to seize the moment and become a master of time and space.

Once you have learned to enter this state of heightened consciousness, you will be able to enter a state of timelessness, where almost anything you can conceive is possible. You must first position yourself to enter this state of heightened consciousness, however. Unless you learn to focus your perceptive awareness and enter this state of heightened consciousness at a moment's notice at will, you will not be able to seize the moment and stretch time. Zen masters and warrior athletes do this all the time, as opportunities arise. It takes practice.

I began to practice after I left the chamber of commerce banquet, where I first learned to control the sounds around me and stop the world to a degree. Flushed from my success, I went on a walk later at dusk in the woods along the river where I lived. At first, I allowed myself to enjoy the sound of the wind through the trees, the rushing of the river, and the chirping of the birds. Then I started to shut down all the sounds around me, muting out the external sounds of nature as well as the internal dialogue inside my own head. When I got very quiet inside my head, I left myself open to whatever might enter the void. For a while, I heard nothing whatsoever and experienced total quiet and calm. Quiet can be beautiful. But what I heard next was incredibly beautiful and most unexpected.

I started to hear what I can only describe as "pan pipes." I had only heard something like this once before, in a recording by the great flutist Jean-Paul Rampal. These riverside pan pipes were even more beautiful and out of this world. This truly was the non-ordinary world; perhaps they really were Pan's pipes. All I know for certain is that I could walk through the woods and modulate the volume of the pan pipes by focusing my attention on them or allowing my focus to wane. I walked through the woods for what seemed like hours, listening to the pan pipes and hearing nothing else. It probably was more like a few minutes at best, because it was fast becoming dark outside. When the woods became very dark, I wandered off for home, dumbstruck by this amazing out-of-this-world experience.

Wonderful things can happen to you when you clear your mind, stop the world, and allow yourself to enter the "now." The present moment is pregnant with potential, if you will open yourself up to it fully. The sacrifices are small. You must be willing to forego the shopping list of haunting memories that lock you into the past, and your concerns that try to trap you into a contrived future. You must be open to the moment at hand and all that it offers you. You must seize the moment.

In this special state of heightened awareness, you may experience insight from your own higher consciousness, receive higher wisdom from the universal intelligence around you, or even step outside of yourself and explore a non-ordinary world of unlimited possibilities. In this state of heightened awareness, you will experience a personal sense of timelessness. Mystics and warrior athletes have been doing this for years. All it requires is discipline and practice.

You may want to try various meditation exercises to start you on your way. To simplify things a bit, I suggest a few meditation techniques that have always worked very well for me.

"Fade to Black" Meditation Exercise

You'll need:
- A straight-back chair
- A quiet, dimly lit room
- Solitude

Directions

Close the door to the room, so you can be quietly alone. Remove your shoes and sit erect in the chair with good upright posture and hands open (palms upright) on your legs. Get comfortable. Relax into a meditative state of mind by clearing your mind of internal thought and chatter. Close your eyes. Tune out any external noises or distractions. Begin to take deep, regular breaths. Allow your body to become numb. Let your mind go blank. As your mind goes blank, picture a clean slate in your mind's eye. Concentrate on seeing a black slate. Everything comes out of darkness. Start with darkness and wait to see what comes next. Do not anticipate anything. Simply stare at the black screen. It won't necessarily pop up instantly, but may take a while to appear to you. It's all up to you. Once you see the black slate, be open to what comes next. This is an opportunity for great insight and personal discovery.

Did you see the black slate in your mind's eye? It might not appear to you the first time you try. If you have difficulty with this approach, you might try picturing a white board instead, the kind of white board used for writing with colored grease pencils. Once you see the slate, you begin to might begin to see things written on the slate, things important to you. Your higher consciousness or soul might be speaking to you. Or perhaps you are receiving information outside yourself. Did you see anything on your slate? Keep trying. This is not the only way to meditate, but it's a good way to start.

"Stopping the World" Exercise

You'll need:
- Many people gathered together
- Many conversations or activities going on at once in a confined area

Step One

This exercise is done in two steps, like the baseball exercise earlier. In the first step, you should observe people's conversations and activities as best you can in ordinary fashion, by simply listening and watching as best you can to see what you can comprehend. (It's important, for the sake of this experiment, that many people be talking at once in a confused, noisy atmosphere, similar to what you might find at a party or social gathering.) Stand more or less in the middle of the group and look around, trying as best you can to understand what people are saying and doing.

Step Two

In the second step, remain in the middle of the group with the noise and confusion the same as before. For the sake of the experience, in fact, it would be ideal if you simply stayed in the same location and did the second step of this experiment immediately after doing step one. In short, this is a continuation of the same confused scene. In this step, however, you should attempt to focus your attention on only one person talking at a time. Try to tune out everything else. You will need to shift your awareness and enter a heightened state of consciousness. Quiet yourself. Focus intently on one of the people talking. Project your personal energy to that person, as though you were hooking on to them like a magnet. Project your energy from your will center. Picture it leaving your body from the region of your abdomen. Listen with your head, not your ears. Concentrate on the person you are watching speak. See and hear nothing else. Tune out everything else.

Were you successful in "stopping the world" around you and selectively focusing your sensory perception? This requires great discipline and practice, but is something you can learn to do to your great personal advantage.

CHAPTER 5

Being two places at once

Is it really possible to be in two places at once? A linear approach to time makes this seem most improbable. After all, that is not the way time works in the ordinary, physical world. But what about the non-ordinary world? If we were able to enter a non-ordinary world through a shift in our perceptive awareness in the manner previously discussed, could we possibly experience two realities that occur simultaneously?

The accounts of Louis Gittner, who said he visited people while meditating in a reclining position, inspired me to consider the possibilities of personal bilocation. Of course, these were only his experiences, based on his own personal perspective. While I found them compelling, I had to admit that they did not carry the same weight with me as personal observation based on my own experience. I had never experienced anything like that before. That situation, however, was about to change.

In the early 1980s, I had an experience in bilocation that changed my life forever. I was living in Oregon, but longed to be back on Orcas

Island to visit the Outlook Inn where Gittner lived. I longed for it so much that I visited there in a meditative state. Meditating one day, I thought I had cleared my mind of all thoughts. My strong desire to be at Orcas Island, however, willed me to be there. As my body went numb and my mind started to clear in reaching a state of heightened awareness, I realized that I had brought one thought with me into mediation—visiting the Outlook Inn. That's very much like what hypnotherapists call a "hypnotic suggestion."

As I entered a meditative state, my blank screen was suddenly filled with a photo-real image of the Outlook Inn the way it would look from the road when you are approaching. It was the front-entrance view. It was raining lightly, which is a little unusual for the San Juan Islands. It seemed a little dark, too. The front door grew closer to me. Then I realized that I had walked to the front door. I looked at the door handle to the front door to the inn. I reached out with a hand and grabbed the door knob. I turned the knob to open the door, but had the sensation that I simply passed through the door. Inside, things looked very different than the way the Outlook Inn had looked to me the last time I had vacationed there. The lobby was rearranged and freshly painted. There was a little, protective cord that blocked off part of the entry. It didn't look quite right to me. Yet, it looked very real.

All at once, I was pulled back to my physical, ordinary world in Oregon with a jerk that I felt deep within my abdomen. It left me feeling a little dazed and disoriented for a brief spell. When I stood up, I realized that my room back in Oregon had grown dark. How long had I been gone? It seemed like only a second.

Later that summer, I visited the Outlook Inn on Orcas Island with family. We piled up the car, took the state ferry to the island, and parked outside the inn. The first thing I noticed when I walked inside the inn was that the entrance had been recently painted and that the lobby was rearranged from the last time we had stopped there. When I mentioned to Gittner that I had visited his inn in a meditative state and seen the remodeling months earlier when the new paint was still fresh, he seemed unimpressed. He added that he did that sort of thing all the time and that it was rather commonplace to him. Still, to me, it was a revelation in human potential. I had visited Orcas Island and witnessed things in vivid detail while meditating in a room in Oregon. In a real sense, I had been in two places at the same time.

Flushed with success, I began to experiment with bilocation more and more. The new feeling of heightened awareness and astral experiences outside the body was so exhilarating to me that I began to pop in and pop out of this state more and more throughout the day. I would even do it while working or walking along the street, because my strong desire willed me to enter that exotic state of being, It was simply more exciting to me than existing all day long in what now seemed a boring world of ordinary reality. At least, that's how I felt at the time. It was like discovering a magic elixir; and I couldn't get enough of it.

Once when I was developing film in our Oregon newspaper's darkroom, I sat down quietly in the dark in a chair with the can of film in one hand and one eye on the film timer. It was set for eight minutes of developing time, as I recall. I stared at the clock and got very relaxed in the chair. I told myself to relax, that I would be there awhile in that chair. The next thing I knew, I was climbing up a mountain somewhere in Tibet. I climbed up and up, as though determined to get somewhere. When I finally returned to my physical body in the ordinary world, the time on the clock had expired. The buzzer on the timer that goes off when time has expired woke me out of my meditative state. I began to worry about the film. How long had I been gone? How much overexposed was the film? Unfortunately, I was not wearing a watch to check the elapsed time in any way. Luckily, the film was somewhat useable, because it's pretty hard to retake accident photos for the newspaper. So I must have been gone five or ten minutes. But I was pretty shocked by how easily I had slipped into a meditative state and left my body.

You'd think that scare with the film in the darkroom would have made me more cautious. But I was like a kid in a candy store, unable to keep my hand out of this new, exciting jar of treats. My next scare happened on the street and could have been fatal.

I remember walking down the main street of our little Oregon town one summer day. I can even remember what I was wearing. It was a nice suit and recently polished dress shoes. I remember how good I felt as I started out walking down the block at the far end of town. It was such a nice day that I had decided to walk the length of the town and make my rounds for the newspaper, leaving my car parked at the office. One minute I was walking down the street, thinking how relaxed I felt. My body was so limber and loose in the fine summer weather. In midstride, my consciousness left my body. Suddenly I was on a beach. It appeared to be Greece; and by the appearance of the ancient sailing vessels and clothing of the people, it was a much earlier time. I remember walking along the beach, then sitting down to watch the boats and the people. It was fascinating. Then I realized that was only visiting and not like the other people there. I realized that I was having an out-of-body experience.

With a sudden jerk, I was back in my body. I was still walking on the sidewalk and almost tripped when my consciousness returned to my physical body on the Oregon street. I was amazed to realize that I had walked a block or two down the street in this sort of meditative trance and wondered how I had done this without any accident. I believe that I even crossed an intersection with cars and passed other people. I was close to the other end of town near our newspaper office. Apparently, I had just slipped out of my body all of a sudden without warning and then returned just as quickly. I estimated that a minute or two had passed as I walked on "automatic pilot" down the sidewalk. On the beach in Greece, however, I had the sensation that I spent several hours walking along the sand and watching the ancient sailing boats in the harbor.

I worried that I was losing control. Looking at this situation and my earlier fiasco in the darkroom, one was tempted to say that I had experienced some sort of momentary blackout. I mean, the visions of the mountain in Tibet and the harbor in Greece were simply daydreams, right? That's the way most people would explain it. All I knew was that these sorts of adventures were happening to me more and more without warning. They could be dangerous, if I were walking in traffic or trying to do critical work at the same time.

So in my inexperience with these matters, I asked a doctor to give me a checkup. He said I looked fine. I suggested to him that I go into the hospital for tests. The doctor said he didn't think that was necessary. I went into the hospital anyway, just to be on the safe side. Curiously, the hospital staff gave me pills in the morning to wake up, pills in the afternoon to stay pain-free, and pills in the night to sleep. They wouldn't tell me exactly what the pills were or why I needed them. So I saved them all in a drawer. At the end of three days, a doctor mysteriously appeared and told me they couldn't figure out what was wrong with me. They said that I appeared to be fine, as far as they could tell. So they released me. And to this day, I have no explanation for my non-ordinary reality experiences in the darkroom and on the street other than involuntary and sudden shifts in consciousness.

The trick, I learned, is to employ some measure of control in consciousness shifts. If your consciousness leaves your body in a meditative state in what's often termed an out-of-body experience, then you must safeguard your "body double" or physical self that is left behind without anyone really at the controls.

I suppose that it's possible for somebody to experience full, simultaneous lives in this fashion. History is filled with legends of doppelgangers and astral doubles. Castaneda wrote several autobiographies about his sorcery instructors from the Yaqui Indian tradition in Mexico and how they appeared to interact with people in two different locations at once, without anyone the wiser. Personally, I have never met anyone that I believe had this ability to appear whole and fully functional in two bodies simultaneously. Most people who have out-of-body experiences, it seems, are not visible to most people around them in their astral form. There are exceptions, of course.

I'm aware of only two people who have been able to see me when I am out of the my body in this fashion. One is a teacher that I visit on the astral plane. Apparently he can see me in this state. He meets me along the shoreline in Greece. The place where he meets me isn't as curious as the time he meets me, however. It's not contemporary time, but Greece the way it looked thousands of years ago. I have reached this conclusion based on the clothes worn by the people there, and the way the civilization appears to me. I think it's the time and place where my teacher last lived a physical life. His consciousness is still alive today, nonetheless, and seems to move around quite freely, or maybe I should confirm that there is no time in this state of consciousness. There is no normal passing of time and no fixed time that locks a person into a certain period.

My astral teacher seems to have normal bodily functions. He picks up things and walks around with me, showing me things. I would consider him a master of life, because he seems very knowledgeable about the nature of the universe. He is very willing to share this information with me and answer my questions.

While my teacher and I are able to see each other and interact bodily in this state of heightened consciousness, it's odd that the other people I see in these settings do not appear to notice me or interact with me in any way. To them, I must seem a phantom. I believe that they can see my teacher, however, because I have seen him interact with other people.

I have interacted with another person in "dreamwalking." This experience is somewhat like Native American shamanic spirit journeys into other worlds. In these shamanic journeys, the spiritual leader of the tribe would leave his physical body and enter the spirit world to gain knowledge for his people. To enter this spirit world, the dreamwalker would first put himself into an altered state of heightened consciousness.

One of the first times I tried dreamwalking, I selected a partner to walk with me in this altered state of consciousness. We laid down together and attempted what might otherwise be called "shared dreaming." We did this along the Salmon River on Mt. Hood in Oregon one spring night in 1982. In this altered state, we were both conscious of standing together along the river and looking down at our bodies by the rocks. Then we were frightened to see a man approaching. It was a fisherman, carrying a rod and tackle. He wore hip-wading boots, a vest, and a cap filled with artificial flies as lures. He pushed back the brush in front of the section of the river where we were and then stopped. Strangely, he didn't seem to see us looking at him, but was responding to something he saw all the same.

The next thing we knew, we were suddenly back in our reclining bodies lying on the river's edge. We sat up with a start and looked at each other knowingly for the time we had shared in this altered state. Then we looked up at the brush. Indeed, a fisherman stood poised with his rod, wading boots, tackle, and cap. He stared down at us. That's what had caught his eye.

"Oh, I'm sorry, " he said. "I didn't want to wake you. Didn't expect to find anyone down here this morning, at least not sleeping down here. Weren't you cold sleeping down here?"

We just smiled. We weren't aware of any discomfort during the night by the river. Later, we discussed what we had seen and experienced the night before in this altered state of consciousness. It was remarkable how our stories matched perfectly and how we had been able to interact somewhat, as we were conscious of each other.

I believe you'd have to concede that a lot of the time during our dreams we do actually go somewhere. By that, I mean that our consciousness leaves our bodies and visits other settings and other situations. Unbound by laws of the physical universe, our consciousness even visits other times and other places. In a sense, that makes all of us masters of time and space. The trick to becoming a full-fledged master of time and space is to have control over these non-ordinary experiences. Most of the time when this sort of thing happens to us, we gush and glow and say how lucky we were and wonder how to have it happen to us again. We are lucky passengers, not drivers in control.

Many people throughout time have claimed to engage in controlled out-of-body experiences, most frequently referred to as "astral projection" or "soul travel." For centuries, witches have reportedly flown through the air on special broomsticks, which is a fanciful way of describing astral projection, according to D. J. Conway in *Flying Without a Broom*. Indeed, Sybil Leek in *Diary of a Witch* predicted that future space exploration would discover that witches had been to distant worlds first and without use of rocketry.

The ancient art and science of Eckankar encourages spiritual discovery by its students through soul travel. This practice is very much like the approach of yogi masters who enter a meditative state of heightened consciousness and then leave the body. They explore worlds within worlds and realms of creation beyond what we would normally call the ordinary, physical world. Former Eck master Paul Twitchell's books, *The Tiger's Fang* and *The Far Country*, describe personal soul travel that explores various levels of creation. This is the sort of spiritual out-of-body journey of the Eastern samadhi and the Native American shaman. The one thing that all of these mystics have in common, of course, is their perceived ability to be in two places at one time.

American author Jane Roberts launched an international movement with Seth International, which was dedicated, in a sense, to the concept that people are living multiple realities simultaneously. The premise behind the multiple identities is that our consciousness gives birth to thought forms about who we want to be; and our will energizes these thought forms to become real, breathing people. When Sethians refer to meeting their "probable others," they mean physical, breathing human beings. As they journey throughout the day and go through their lives, Sethians look for their "probable others" in hopes of bumping into them. These are the people they breathed into existence, in a sense, and also fed with their energy. They are the athletes they once dreamed of becoming and the artists they simply thought into existence. These artists and athletes that they created are extensions of themselves. They are alternate realities of who they intended to become. Sethians love to spot themselves in a crowd and love to play "dress up" at conventions to explore their alternate realities.

Sorcerers of old feared coming face-to-face with their doppelgangers or astral doubles. Such astral travelers would try not to look into the eyes of their physical selves. This is very different from the Sethians who seek out their probable others. Admittedly, the Sethians are not talking about astral bodies as nonmaterial doubles, but rather physical doubles who are living their alternate reality in the physical world.

Generally one's astral body during out-of-body travel cannot be seen by most people. In fact, the first few times you attempt astral travel, you might have trouble distinguishing your own astral body. The astral body is the emotional, energy body that surrounds the physical body. It is a subtle body that all living creatures including all animals, plants, and people have surrounding their denser, physical body. You might think of it as an etheric body. As such, it is nonphysical.

To see it at all requires vision beyond that of normal, physical eyesight. It would require a conscious awareness to discern it. People who can see or read auras around people and other living things can see the astral body. This requires heightened consciousness and much practice to do. It's something that you can definitely learn to do, however. Practice looking at people who are stationed in front of a window. Don't stare at them directly, but rather look at them sort of sideways, shifting your eyes to see them. It's sort of a sideways glance, usually out of the corner of your left eye. You will begin to be conscious of a soft, white glow around people's physical bodies, when you first attempt to see their auras. Then you begin to interpret the light that surrounds them and assign colors to them. The colors are seen inside your third eye, not with your physical eyes. You reflect on the aura surrounding a person and then "feel" inside you what the true colors of these light emanations are.

Our concern here is not interpreting the colors of these energy emanations in the human aura, but rather becoming conscious of the presence of the subtle bodies that surround the physical self (see Figure 2, following page). The astral body that surrounds you is your health aura, your etheric double. It is directly linked to the physical body and fits with it like an envelope that encapsulates an important letter. The astral body, when seen for the first time in out-of-body travel, might appear larger than the physical body it normally surrounds. It might appear slightly more grotesque than the physical body with which it is associated. It also has powers beyond that of the physical body, since it is not bound by time and space. It's most at home in the astral world of non-ordinary reality, an alternate reality that is decidedly nonphysical.

I believe the basic distinctions between astral travel and the soul travel described in Eckankar is that Eck attempts to send the person's soul outside of this world into other, higher realms for spiritual discovery. Astral travel takes the astral body of the person into astral worlds that are more bound to this level of creation, near to our physical world. In Eckankar, therefore, a subtle body other than the astral body leaves the person on a rather exotic journey of discovery, a journey of the higher soul.

There are exercises to help you leave your body. We have seen, of course, how you might be able to leave the body as an extension of normal meditation. Some people nonetheless find consciously leaving the body in a waking meditative state sometimes difficult. There are shortcuts. I have found these specific techniques to be sure-fire methods for me to journey out-of-body. Because I have personally tested these techniques and know that they work for me, I recommend them to you.

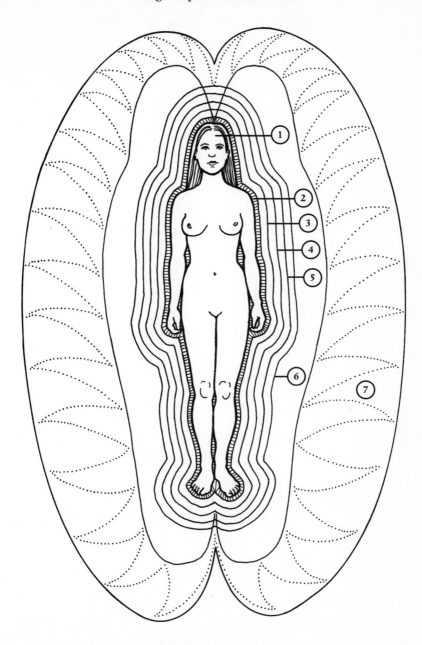

Figure 2 • SUBTLE BODIES
1 – Physical Body 2 – Astral Body (Emotions) 3 – Mental Body (Rational Thought)
4 – Causal Body (Insight) 5 – Individualized Consciousness
6 – Energized Conscious Awareness 7 – Divine Essence

Kaleidoscope Meditation Technique
to Stimulate Leaving the Body

You'll need:

- Quiet room
- Comfortable position—either sitting or reclining on your back (I prefer being on my back)
- Some light in the room is best (or, at least, not a dark room)

Directions

This is inspired by my study in Eckankar. The technique is designed to "stop the world" in the sense that you attempt to selectively control your sensory perceptions.

Lie on your back or sit quietly. Attempt to quiet your mind and shut out outside distractions, so you can enter a meditative state. Concentrate on making your body go numb, as though entering a sleep state. Keep your mind alert, but not focused on any thought or distraction. Become conscious of your breathing and begin to take deeper, longer breaths.

Now picture a red light inside your mind's eye. Let it come into focus so that you see it very well and feel the intensity of the bright, red color. Hold the color in your head for a moment. Now get ready to play kaleidoscope. Switch the color slowly to orange. When you feel that you can see the orange brightly in your mind's eye, then let it dissolve into yellow. Wait until the soft, fuzzy yellow becomes a rich yellow color. Hold the yellow color in your mind's eye and focus on it. Now repeat the process again, starting with red. This time make the transitions faster in your mind's eye. Red comes into focus quickly, then fades into bright orange. Then orange gives way to yellow. Do the exercise over and over, but faster each time. The colors must be distinct and bright. If they are not, slow down until your can better focus. This is an exercise in heightened awareness and sharpening your personal power. You are getting ready to launch out of your body.

As you race through the color switches in your mind's eye, you will eventually find the color slate in front of you turning black. Don't panic. When the colors disappear and you see the black slate, you are ready to leave the body. Things should happen pretty much on their own naturally from that point. (In my experience, somebody usually grabs me and pulls me out of my body at this point. Eckists might call this an Eck master or spiritual guide. You might think of it as your guardian angel. It's a friendly spirit to help you.) Once you have mastered the technique of out-of-body travel, you might simply leave your body on your own at this point, after the bright red, orange, and yellow colors fade to black.

People can leave their bodies painlessly. When you return, however, you might feel a sort of snap, probably felt in your abdomen. Most people lead from their will center in leaving their body, which means that they are projecting energy from their bodies from the region of their solar plexus. There is nothing particularly dangerous about this. Have a nice adventure and try to recall everything that you encounter and learn in your out-of-body travel. This is a spiritual journey of discovery.

Reverse Belly Flop Technique

This is the technique inspired by the writings of Carlos Castaneda. The author's Yacqui Indian teacher would attempt to shift the student's awareness with whacks on the lower back to manipulate what he called "assemblage points" on the spine. We might think of this as stimulating the chakras that run along the spinal column. The chakras, according to Hindu and Buddhist teachings, are swirling vortexes of energy that govern various activities in the body (see Figure 3, page 68). In translating these seven major chakras to traditional Western medicine, the seven energy vortexes correspond roughly to the endocrine glands in the human physical body.

I have found that I can stimulate a sudden shift in my perceptive awareness and enter a state of heightened attention without having somebody whack me on my lower back. I simple flop down on a hard bed, leading with my lower back. I call this my "reverse belly flop," because it usually makes a big splash of a sort.

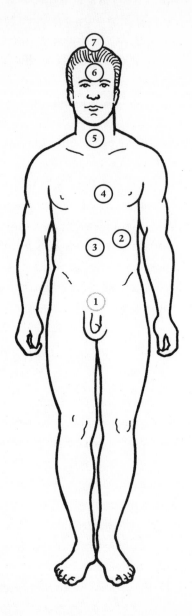

Figure 3 • SEVEN MAJOR CHAKRAS
1 – Root Chakra 2 – Spleen Chakra 3 – Navel Chakra 4 – Heart Chakra
5 – Throat Chakra 6 – Brow Chakra 7 – Crown Chakra

The first time I did this, I instantly left my body and was suddenly conscious of hovering over my body on the bed. I began to float higher and higher above the bed and floated through the roof of the house and into the trees. Soon I was floating through the sky high above my little community. It was exhilarating, very vivid, and so sudden that I wasn't quite prepared to deal with it all. I quickly snapped back into the safe confines of my physical body.

Since this first encounter, I have learned that many people use a technique something like this. It does seem rather safe. It jolts you out of your body. All I suggest is that you be prepared to leave the room rather quickly and learn to fly. You will need to know. Like anything else, it requires focused intent, will power, and practice.

CHAPTER 6

Remote viewing, astral travel, distance healing, and exploring exotic realms

I'll never forget the horrible day when Ben, one of my cats, was hit by a car. She was struck in such a way that two critical bones were broken, making it impossible for her to walk. She could only drag the lower half of her little body around. It was really pathetic to watch. The way her pelvis and femur were shattered, my vet said that it wasn't even operable unless I took the cat across the country to some special hospital in New England or maybe let the local university try something radical.

It really seemed that time had run out for this little Tonkanese cat, which was especially sad for the limited life she had led. I rescued her from a basement where she had been abused and neglected by her alcoholic owner, who first found her abandoned in an alley as a kitten. He would paw her awkwardly when drunk and then throw her against the wall or hold her under the shower if she didn't like the way he petted her. When her owner would pass out for a day or two, Ben would have nothing to eat or drink. When I rescued her from the basement where she lived, I noticed claw marks on the walls where she'd tried in vain to jump out of the basement windows. They were never open to her.

So I felt especially sorry for her when she was hit by a car in two places and wasn't expected to live. The veterinarian said that her chances in such an operation were not good and that she'd probably need to be "destroyed." He told me to bring her back in about a week, so he could reassess her chances. You could just tell that he was humoring me and trying to buy time for what he probably thought was the logical conclusion—euthanasia.

To make matters even worse with regard to the horrible timing of this, my new job for an international book publisher was going to take me out of the country for a full week. I wouldn't be there to monitor the little cat's condition and bring her to the doctor for the follow-up assessment. So I asked a kindly neighbor lady and her fiancé to check on my cat several times a day and take her back to the vet in about five days or sooner if necessary.

What could I do from such long distance? I felt so hopeless. Then I remembered Karen, the healer I had met through Mt. Hood Hospice back in Oregon. She was an empathic healer with amazing success in distance healing. I had heard that this sort of thing was possible. I remembered that an Indian yogi master named Sri Sai Baba also was credited with healing people by long distance. Witches, too, have been reported to practice distance healing. But I had actually seen my friend Karen do it, and so I was a true believer. I recalled how she would send through the mail healing rocks charged with her healing touch to energize people. I had also stood by her on a street corner and seen her assess sick people across the road and then send them healing energy without ever meeting them. If Karen could heal strangers, and Sai Baba could heal his devoted followers throughout the world, why couldn't I help this poor little cat?

I decided to visit Ben in my astral body to help affect her healing process. Twice a day, I would lie on my bed in London and project my astral double to this little, broken cat lying helplessly in a box back in the United States. I could see the cat so clearly that I knew I was getting through to her and helping her. I remember her startled face the first time she realized I was in the room attempting to help her. She was very cooperative. Because the astral body is not limited by the laws of the physical universe, the mending of the leg was magical and not medical in the traditional sense.

Because the astral body is associated with the health aura and emotional field that intertwines with the physical body, it can comfortably interact with the physical body and energize it to begin the healing process. I know that this is true, because I have done it. I saw no other way to help heal Ben.

The Tonkanese feline had been a bit shy around people even after I rescued her from her abusive owner. But she was willing let me reach out to her and touch her with my astral body. I ran energy from my astral body throughout her little body, drawing from the energy around me. Then I reached inside her body and mended the broken bones. Every day I repeated this out-of-body experience. Every day I visited little Ben and practiced distance healing in this fashion. I tried very hard to believe that the remote healing was working. I did not speak with the woman who was caring for the cat for the entire week, since she was always away at work when I was able to call. So I had to wait a week to learn how my cat was doing.

The results were miraculous. When I returned, the neighbor said that Ben started to pick up spirits a little after the second day and then seemed able to move around a little after about four days. She took Ben to the vet on the sixth day for a reassessment to determine whether the cat might benefit from the tricky operation or was hopelessly crippled. The vet was astounded, according to my neighbor. At first, he didn't think it was the same cat. He took x-rays of Ben's two broken bones. They were mended. He sent Ben home without any further treatment.

There's only one curious last detail to the story. The cat's bones are fused in a slightly odd manner. Admittedly, I did not know anatomy when I jumped in to help. Neither did little Ben. Today the little Tonkanese races around the neighborhood and climbs trees with the agility of a squirrel. But when I pet her hind section, we are both conscious of the fact that two bones don't fit together in the normal fashion. Nonetheless, both the cat and I see her as healthy and strong. This is our shared perception and now a part of our functional reality.

Despite the slight irregularity in her mended bones, she is not shy at all around me, as she once was. Rather, she seems to welcome my touch. She remains somewhat shy around all other people and other cats, however. She will not permit other people to touch her hind quarters, or pick her up. This is just one example of distance healing in which a person in an out-of-body state remotely views something in the physical world. There are other ways to do this.

Distance healing is possible without astral travel. Many natural healers claim success healing with thought forms. The thought forms must be focused with your intent and energized by your will. The major difference between this and astral healing is that your astral double does not leave your physical body. Consequently, your etheric double is not involved in direct manipulations at the location of the injured party you wish to visit in distance healing. Hence, you do not scan and survey the injured party on location. Healing by long distance with this approach might require some prior knowledge of the precise extent of the injury, since you will not remotely view it in an astral body. You are simply sending thought forms.

Thought forms can be very powerful. The honored doctor and researcher Andrija Puharich determined, in tests with gifted psychic Uri Geller, that a person's focused thought forms could bend metal or heal. As a visible demonstration of the power of thought forms, Geller would bend metal spoons on cue. I have seen less-famous people demonstrate this, too—one a Cuban-American friend named Domingo Piniero, and another a group of Theosophists at Camp Indralaya in the San Juan Islands.

Puharich found that the frequency of thought forms varied according to application, and that a harmonic frequency of the energy wave generated by thought forms, and fed by willful intent, could match the harmonic frequency of the Earth and healthful life. A harmonic frequency that matches the resonance of the Earth and the natural healthy state of living beings would restore health to an injured or ill subject, he said. A different (lower) frequency to your thought forms, if energized by willful intent and focused, could bend metal. Obviously, our thought forms, when energized and focused, can become directed energy.

Franz Anton Mesmer (1734–1815), from whose name we derive the term *mesmerize*, used to fill a tub of water and then magnetize it with his healing hands. This is similar to a Puharich experiment, during which Uri Geller handled a glass filled with water, projecting his energy at just the right healing frequency. The water would maintain this frequency for some time.

I recall my friend Karen, the psychic healer in Oregon, doing a similar thing. She would hold a quartz crystal in one hand, loading it with healing energy. Then she would put that crystal into a jar of water and place the jar outside in the moonlight. Later the next day, she would remove the crystal and give the water to someone to drink, if she happened to know anyone sick or down in the dumps at the time. It always seemed to me that the water from Karen's crystal jar was softer and sweeter than any other water I have ever tasted. And, yes, it did seem to work. At least, that was my perceptive reality. The other thing I remember about Karen's crystal water is that it "tingled" as you drank it, as though energized.

The question that begs asking, perhaps, is just how much of one's human consciousness leaves the body during the sending of thought forms? It would seem possible to be in two places at the same time without sending an astral double, or having an out-of-body experience. The mental body, like the astral body, is one of the subtle bodies in the classical Hindu model. Like the astral body, the mental body has its own chakra energy associated with it. The mental realm is a world reality just as real as the physical world; it's just that it's completely mental in orientation and not physical in form. There is so much more to us than meets the eye. Our levels of reality seem layered like an onion with its many layers of skin.

If you are a parent, perhaps you can recall instances where you have practiced a sort of remote viewing to check your child's safety on occasion. You probably didn't even think much about it at the time, because it seemed so natural to you. But perhaps you had the momentary sensation that your body was floating through the neighborhood haunts where your children might be found, looking across yards and playgrounds to spot your child. When you thought you saw your child, you were suddenly back at your job, with a jolt. Or if you couldn't find your child as you scanned the neighborhood haunts, you felt uneasy throughout the day and worried about your child.

Indeed, parents' desire to see their children and their intent to guard them are so powerfully focused that their consciousness leaves their bodies at will. These parents might be at work, but their consciousness from time-to-time travels across great distances in just an instant to periodically check on their children's safety. It's only natural, just as a mother's kiss on a children's skinned elbow is the best medicine in the world.

I know that when my son was growing up and playing in the neighborhood, I would think of him and worry about him greatly throughout the day. Unable to go look for him all of the time, I would project myself to where I thought he might be. I remember looking down alleys, in neighbors' yards, and up trees many times, without ever leaving my place at work. I'll bet a lot of parents do that. One minute you're at work, staring at the task in front of you, then the next minute, you're floating throughout the neighborhood, scanning everywhere for your child. In a real sense, then, most parents have been in two places at the same time, or have bilocated. After all, a parent pretty much has to be in two places all the time to raise a kid safely these days.

Many people treat their pets like their children, and probably do the same bilocation trick in checking up on their wandering pooches and felines throughout the day. Animal behaviorist and author Beatrice Leidecker apparently does this with her dog friends. She tells the story of worrying about a group of dogs that she "saw" breaking out of their individual kennels at the animal shelter she had just visited. She was driving her car during this insightful vision. She saw that they had gotten together and were about to engage in a big fight at the shelter. These dogs normally were kenneled separately, since the larger and more aggressive dogs couldn't be trusted to share quarters with some of the more timid dogs. Leidecker felt certain from her vision that some of her dogs were about to fight.

She had just left the shelter, however, and was miles down the road in her car at the time. Since she was unable to drive back quickly enough and sensed immediate danger, she sent her thoughts to the dogs that she would be very angry with them and would discipline them if they fought. She acted out for them some exaggerated disciplinary action she might take in retaliation. When she finally arrived by car, she found that the dogs had indeed gotten loose, as she had seen. However, they were all sitting very quietly and obediently on far sides of the one big area they all shared. Something had discouraged them from mixing it up, as one would have ordinarily expected.

Perhaps the biggest scare I ever had as a parent was the day I sensed that my six-year-old boy had met with deadly danger while playing. I remember that I was working at the newspaper, wondering just how my son was doing playing with the neighbor boy. We lived in a waterfront town beside city docks where people moored their boats. The neighbor boy lived across the street. In my mind, I considered where my son might be. In my mind, I was unable to determine a satisfactory answer. The next thing I knew I sort of blanked out for a moment and felt my consciousness leave my body. Some people might call this a daydream. This was different, however. I had this vivid experience of visiting the neighbor boy's home and racing through all of the rooms to his house and across his backyard very quickly, seeing things in great detail all at once. I was scanning everything for my son. Where was he? I did not see him there. I continued to race throughout the neighborhood. Suddenly, I was at the city docks. There I saw two boys. One was wearing an orange life jacket. It was my son.

I panicked! My son was playing on the city floats. I saw that he was wearing an orange life preserver. This must mean danger. I returned back to my physical body with a jolt. I shook my head to clear my thoughts, which were pretty muddled and frightened by the images I had seen. I ran out the door, looking for my son.

I nearly bumped into him outside the front door. He was just returning home. And, yes, he had been playing near the city floats. In fact, he told me that he had been playing with the neighbor boy that I had seen with him in my vision. My son said that he just wanted to check in with me to let me know that he was okay. I didn't ask him for any more details. I was just relieved to see him standing there.

If you ever served in the military or had someone close to you who did, you probably have a similar story to tell. At times, you may have felt that you were there in the room with your loved one, despite the physical distance between you and the fact that you were somewhere else at the time. Perhaps you could even smell them or see what they were wearing. Perhaps you noticed that they had cut their hair and not told you, or that they had new clothes. Perhaps you were even surprised what you found them doing.

Isn't it a bit odd, for instance, that servicemen or their spouses sometimes know early on that their beloved had been cheating on them, even though they were not there to see it? Sometimes, it's almost as though the jilted lovers had peeked in on them.

Astral journeys can take you to many exotic locations. It rather depends on whether you have enough personal power to get there. Some of the most exotic places have been described in the accounts of Eck master Paul Twitchell in *The Tiger's Fang*. The main character in the story leaves his body in out-of-body soul travel and journeys with a proper spiritual traveler as a guide to distant worlds and levels of creation. He meets the various lords who rule these various planes of existence (which Hindu Vedantists list as astral, mental, wisdom, bliss, and God planes). These planes correspond to the various layers of the human subtle bodies and might be interpreted as astral, causal, mental, soul, and God planes. The seeker journeys to a place above our world that might be described as heaven. It is the top of what is described as the first grand division of the universe, which includes our physical world and the lower astral world below it.

This high astral realm seems to include saints, prophets, religious leaders, angels, and what Christians might call God. But all of this is actually a lower division of the universe, though as high as most of us will ever climb. Above this peak is the second grand division of the universe. There is a bridge that leads from this the top of this heavenly peak to another, higher realm of creation. There one finds another overseer. That world leads to another world with another lord.

Each world has its own strengths and limitations. There is a world where the out-of-body traveler has no emotional body. There is another world, however, where the soul traveler has no mental body. The many layers of our reality are explored in worlds where aspects of our subtle bodies are featured. In the last, highest realm of creation, the soul traveler surveys a vast ocean of love and hears only the word of God as waves that push new souls toward our world. Love of God encourages souls to evolve and eventually return to God like the outgoing tide, the seeker learns. Twitchell's compelling visions of a soul traveler's out-of-body journey throughout all of creation corresponds to the sort of mystic out-of-body meditations experienced by mystic Hindu yogis.

My own attempts at soul travel to these higher realms of creation have been pretty rough journeys, I'm afraid. In my first trip to the top of the first grand creation, I saw angels sitting on what looked like street corners and encountered a waterfall. The waterfall, I was told, represented a sort of life force sent down to the physical world below.

Near the waterfall, I found a huge sandbox with a huge throne at the front of the sandbox. I started to walk in the sandbox to approach the tall chair for a better look, and found walking in the sand very difficult.

I had been brought there by a spirit guide with long, dark hair, a wonderful nature-loving spirit named Selena (at least she told me I could call her that, when I asked her name). My guide discouraged me from approaching the throne of the lord of heaven. She said that I was in great danger and was not prepared. She was probably right.

The person who sat on the throne looked like a man. He asked me what right I had to be there. I told him who I was. He told me that he was the one and only God and that there was no God above him. I answered something to the effect that I was surprised, because he didn't strike me as the all-powerful, all-knowing lord of creation. He told me not to go any further. Against the strong advice of my guide, who was beginning already to abandon me in my folly, I scoffed at this lord of heaven and started to walk toward a bridge.

On the bridge, I found many souls attempting to walk to the other side. It was more difficult than it appeared. I must confess that I have never really crossed that bridge in out-of-body travel. I often have wondered if I would experience the other realms of higher creation and lords as Twitchell and the Indian samadhi mystics have reported in their journeys.

There are exercises that I have found helpful in setting up remote viewing and astral healing; and I would like to share these out-of-body techniques with you.

Remote Viewing Exercise

You'll need:
- Quiet, isolated room
- Clean place to recline (bed, mat, or clean floor)

Directions

Recline on your back (or sit in a straight-back chair, with your bare feet firmly planted on the ground). Allow yourself to enter a state of heightened awareness by letting your body go to sleep and keeping your mind superattentive. Close your eyes. Clear your mind of internal and external distractions.

Picture a black screen in your mind's eye. As the black screen begins to come into focus, consider where you want to go. Pick a place or person you want to visit. Picture that person or place on the screen in front of you. See them clearly the way you expect them to actually look at this moment if you were to visit them. See them in their actual setting.

Now will yourself to be in that picture and project your energy from the will center in the abdominal part of your body. Feel the energy pulling you along. See yourself now in the picture. Now dissolve your attention to yourself in the picture. Leave your physical body. *Be* the visitor in the picture. See things there with great detail. Look around carefully to see things with clarity of focus. Look at your own hands to establish to your own satisfaction that you are actually there. Now watch the person or subject you came to visit. Observe them carefully and with great detail. Try very hard to hear what they are saying. Try to pick up what they are thinking. Watch their hands and feet move. Notice what they are doing. What color clothes are they wearing? What is their body language saying? Do they look well? Be an excellent witness.

(Note: If you have trouble meditating and seeing the blank slate in your mind's eye, then try using the kaleidoscope technique described earlier in chapter 5. Try picturing a flashing sequence of bright red, orange, and yellow light in your mind's eye, before fading to a black screen. If you are still having trouble fading to a blank screen in your meditation, then try fluttering your eyes rapidly and holding them tightly shut to trigger the flashing light. Concentrate on focused intent to make the light turn colors in flashing rotation. This happens in your mind's eye. You will need to concentrate and use your creative imagination.

If you have trouble leaving the body, try flopping down on your back on a soft mat or bed, leading with your lower back. Be careful not to injure yourself, but concentrate of shocking your subtle body to leave your physical body. You might want to review the earlier exercise titled "Reverse Belly Flop Technique" in chapter 5.)

Astral Healing Exercise

You'll need:
- Quiet, isolated room for meditation
- A straight-back chair or mat for reclining on your back

Directions

Enter a meditative state as previously outlined. As you are about to enter a deep meditative state and begin to fade to blankness with a blank screen in your mind's eye, give yourself the directive to visit someone who is ill. Focus your intent and direct your will center to energize this single purpose. Leave the body in the manner previously outlined. See yourself beside the subject that you intended to visit and desired to help. Now look at your hands. Be aware of your presence beside this person who needs your help. Perhaps it is a pet. Perhaps it is a sick aunt or good friend who is ailing.

Listen to what she is saying. Hear her thoughts. Observe the illness that is troubling her. To do this, visualize the energy swirls around her body. Look for gaps or broken spaces where light does not surround her body brightly. Look for dark spots around them, where there appears to be something like a gray or dark fog surrounding the body. Reach into that fog. Project your energy into her body, revitalizing it. If you know the anatomical source of the problem that ails her, reach that spot. Your astral hands will penetrate her body. You can reach inside her. Project healing thoughts and energy into the body. Reach into her with your focused intention and will, and intend her to be well. Project a healing vibration into her. Make it feel the way you feel when you feel wonderful and most healthy. Pass that on to your friend here. Desire that your friend be well. Will this person to be well. Let your energy touch your friend's energy. Jumpstart this person's battery.

CHAPTER 7

Our universe is flat, three-dimensional, and just around the bend from other universes

Is there any hard evidence for parallel realities and additional dimensions outside a mystic's adventures into non-ordinary reality? Science has always sought an answer to that question. Now many cutting-edge physicists believe they have a positive answer. Physicists, of course, seek to create a picture of reality as we should see it outside ourselves. Their theories are naturally abstract, but based in scientific research into the nature of things.

What some of the most celebrated modern physicists have to say about parallel worlds and additional dimensions is really astounding. They say that parallel realities with additional dimensions do indeed exist, but that they exist in entirely different universes. Furthermore, these uncharted universes run parallel to our universe.

The big picture they describe looks like a folded map. Our entire universe and our limited reality exist on one side of the folded map. On the other side of the map, a parallel universe exists just beyond our reach. In fact, they say that it might be correct to think of a road map folded many times, with many parallel universes and many additional dimensions on the other sides of the folds.

They say that our own universe is a rather flat place just around the bend from parallel universes, but limited basically by our three visible dimensions. That's the conclusion of several leading physicists who collaborated recently on a breakthrough article in *Scientific American* magazine, titled "The Universe's Unseen Dimensions." The article was written by a team of physicists, including Nima Arkani-Hamed, Savas Dimopoulous, and Georgi Dvali. They concluded that the universe where we live and experience life is actually limited. Our visible universe is somewhat like a thin membrane in space with limited dimensions. In fact, they say that our universe may exist on a thin wall in the grand scheme of things. In the limited universe where we live, the dimensions to our existence are restricted to up-down, forward-backward, and left-right.

They see our entire three-dimensional universe as a sort of thin membrane floating in the full space of dimensions—possibly as many as ten dimensions in all. These extra dimensions would help unify forces of nature and could contain parallel universes. They maintain that invisible parallel universes could coexist with ours on spatial membranes less than a millimeter from our own visible universe. A slightly different way of viewing this proximity, they say, is that these invisible, parallel universes might be simply different sheets of our own thin universe, folded back on itself, sort of like a bent wall poster or folded many times over like a road map.

These invisible universes might be totally different from our visible universe, according to these scientists. They might be composed of completely different forces and particles. The scientists also consider it possible that there could exist a parallel universe to ours that has identical properties to our own. They suggest that we begin to view the universe where we live as a flat piece of paper that has been folded a number of times in the extra dimensions.

They say that objects on the opposite side of our fold could appear very distant, even though they are not. Although we are very close to the other side in a sense, we are distant in that light from one side of the fold could take billions of years to reach us, as it works its way around the folds in space. Consequently, parallel universes appears to us to be very far away. This, too, could be a matter of human perception. We are restricted in that we cannot see beyond the immediate three dimensions.

Our inability to see beyond the surface of our known universe has always been a limitation. Our senses, perception, and frame of reference allow us to experience just three dimensions fully. Even our word for these three experienced forces, *dimensions,* demonstrates that we are linear thinkers who must measure distances to the right of us, vertically, and by depth. In fact, we really see in only two dimensions, with our inability to truly comprehend depth perhaps best demonstrated by our bafflement in confronting a cube. By our nature, we measure things. The things we measure in our frame of reference are basically perpendicular angles. We measure point A to point B. We measure up and down to get the full measure of things. Sometimes we attempt to triangulate, or show how three lines intersect. This is how we experience reality. It is limited by our sensory perception and consciousness in our ordinary world.

It is difficult for three-dimensional beings like ourselves to imagine additional dimensions, of course. We are limited by our sensory receptors, our perception, and our experience in our existing frame of reference. We also have consciousness to experience our known reality, but most of us only employ normal consciousness and not the higher consciousness of what mystics and meditators often call "the higher mind." It's hard for most of us to even think beyond the known three dimensions, of course, when our entire experience is limited to a three-dimensional universe. This is our known reality, based on our life experience. We have no other points of reference. It's difficult to think about our universe folded like a map, with another universe on the other side to ours, parallel to our own reality.

To more easily grasp the idea of these added dimensions being stacked together, yet hidden from our view, think about receiving a beautifully wrapped box. It's an incredibly beautiful package with fancy bows and lovely wrapping paper. You thank the giver and remark that it's a beautiful gift. You admire it, fondle it, and even hold it to your ear to listen when you shake it a little. But the giver tells you there is lots more to this present. You have been admiring only the outer packaging. So you remove the wrapping and find another box inside. You open box after box until you get to the core of the complex wrapping. The actual gift was wrapped in the smallest box of all. Removing all of the elaborate wrapping was most revealing to you, and uncovered a total surprise. Each box was perfectly aligned with the next larger box outside it and the next smaller box inside it. From your perspective in first receiving the gift, you had no way to know that you were really holding ten boxes folded together in one tight package.

It might help you to think of each inner box as another dimension to the gift. The gift had many dimensions, all perfectly aligned. Unfortunately, our perception doesn't allow us to see beyond the box. We can't think outside the box.

Russian P. D. Ouspensky, author of *Tertium Organum,* had a similar way to describe dimensions and how the human mind perceives reality. He described our known dimensions as intersecting lines, with each line or plane containing a section of the plane above it. In a real sense, each new dimension is a layer above the preceding one. But there is a problem in perception associated with living on one plane or one dimension and not really experiencing the dimension that intersects yours. You could see only a slice of the dimension that intersects yours. Consequently, a one-dimensional being wouldn't notice anything happening on the next line or plane above it, even though the line or dimension above him intersects his own little world. In fact, a being on this limited plane would probably perceive the slice of the higher plane that intersects his world as a phenomenon of the unknown world beyond his reality. The same would be true of a two-dimensional being whose line or plane is intersected by a third-dimensional line. He cannot see beyond his own two-dimensional reality. The same, it follows, would be true of people as three-dimensional beings who are unable to see beyond our three-dimensional reality, despite the possible close proximity to a fourth or fifth dimension. These mysteries are beyond our limited perception in ordinary reality—just beyond our immediate grasp.

We are surface dwellers restricted to a third-dimensional reality. We cannot look deeply enough to see a fourth dimension or possible dimensions beyond a fourth dimension. That is far different than saying that they don't exist. It is simply saying that they are beyond our immediate grasp in our ordinary experience of reality.

Many people throughout history have postulated that time or time and motion could be our fourth dimension, since we do seem to experience time. But when you really think about it, time is only a contrived method of measurement or a convenience that we invented, according to the philosopher Immanuel Kant. Time is a matter of perception and relative to the person who experiences it.

I know this from living in Alaska. There, Inuits traditionally have experienced time differently from many other people in the fast-paced, urban world. I learned this from an Alaskan schoolteacher. He told me that his Inuit pupils would sincerely promise they would do their homework each night. Every new morning, however, his pupils would have no homework to show him. They insisted that they would do the homework by the following day. But tomorrow never came in the way the teacher expected it. His pupils were not being deceitful. They were not attempting to avoid the work. They simply had a totally different concept of time and what tomorrow meant, based on their perception and experience of time.

Indeed, our handling of time is very cultural, when you think about it. In many parts of the world, a dinner party set to start at 6 P.M. could legitimately start around 7 or even 7:30 P.M. That's just one cultural group's way of handling time. All of us tend to think of a day as twenty-four hours. A day, however, lasts only as long as the sun shines on that part of our world. It's very relative to where you live in the world and the solar season. Finally, clocks were devised to measure time with precision to standardize time for all of us. These mechanical devices were meant to demystify the variable measurement of time. So now our day officially starts at 12:01 A.M.—regardless of whether it's actually day or night where you live. And, of course, it's only 12:01 A.M. in your specific time zone, relative to where you are experiencing time in motion, as we seem to know it. (All of this would seem particularly odd if you were an astronaut on the Moon or Mars, although these new habitats would be considered part of our visible universe, as well. A new standardized time system would be necessary for these locations in our physical universe.)

Time is simply a convenient way we devised to measure change, as we experience it. Many leading physicists today are beginning to believe that time is *not* outside our three dimensions at all. We experience a sense of time, albeit contrived, within our three-dimensional reality.

Physicist Julian Barbour, author of *The End of Time,* says that he's not alone in his belief that time is an illusion and doesn't exist at all. He says that the solar clock is the only clock that matters. The solar day is what governs all life on Earth. Beyond that, time is pretty much a human invention. Barbour agrees with renowned Austrian physicist Ernest Mach that time is an abstraction at which we arrive by means of the changes in things.

For Barbour, the only way we seem to experience time at all is through snapshots that record our memory of an event at any point. What we really experience, he said, are instants. People tend to think of time as endlessly flowing forward, but that's not how we experience it. He points out that almost everyone seems to see time as something linear, as instants strung on an endless line. But the only real time is the Now, similar to the "Eternal Now" of Hindu philosophy. So Barbour sees people experiencing time like passengers on a train, imagining that they are progressing through time. They seem to be moving forward. But are they really? Every stop on the train is a new instant. The Now is everchanging.

Even the way we seem to conceptualize the flow of events in a movie or dance performance is contrived, based actually on independent snapshots or instants that we have recorded and chosen to play in our brains as continuous time in motion. Barbour uses the example of how we might see a gymnast who performs a series of floor exercises. We see and record the position of the gymnast at preceding instants. Our brain, however, can't process data instantaneously. So we encode several, independent images of the performing gymnast. The brain, Barbour said, interprets the collection of snapshots it has encoded and plays them as a motion picture for us. He suggests that the brain in any instant always contains several stills of a movie. It's like those little "flip books" of pictures that show various positions. When you flip through the book of pictures, they appear to demonstrate motion, like a motion picture. What you are really seeing are instants or snapshots played in rapid succession to artificially suggest a continuous flow of motion through time. Is the image moving, or are you simply moving a collection of still pictures to create the illusion of time and motion?

Kant regarded time as a subjective form of our receptivity. He said that we created time ourselves for the convenience of perceiving the outside world. It is the convenient way we devised to measure change, as we seem to experience it. It is not outside our three-dimensions at all, according to Barbour and many of his associates. This is obvious to anyone who plots road trips in a car. You drive sixty miles at a speed of 60 mph and conclude that you "clocked" sixty minutes of driving time. This is the way a linear thinker approaches reality—by putting a measuring stick against everything we see and do.

In truth, we even have trouble seeing three dimensions in our limited universe. We can barely conceptualize a cube, but cannot truly see it without breaking it down to surface angles. We live in a shallow, surface world of limited access. Like the one-dimensional being who couldn't see the plane above him, we cannot see the dimensions above our plane. They are completely outside our physical universe and beyond our grasp.

Perhaps that is the way our early ancestors felt when they would look across the vast oceans in centuries gone by and attempt to fathom distant worlds that were not visible to them. First of all, they looked across what appeared to them to be a flat world as far as the eye could see, believing that eyes could not be deceived. They reasoned that if they traveled far enough straight ahead into the vast, unknown worlds beyond their shores, they would either find new worlds or else fall off the flat Earth trying. Then they figured that they would need to turn around and come home. It never occurred to them, as linear thinkers with a flat-Earth mentality, that they could continue in any direction and eventually return home by circumnavigating the basically round world. Even the greatest looking glasses could not enable ancient mariners to see around the curve in the Earth, after all.

Carlos Castaneda, renowned author and anthropologist, told a similar story about the way Yacqui Indians of ancient Mexico passed down what he called the "sorcerer's explanation" of the world and how they viewed reality. The sorcerers looked at the human eye as the microcosm of the world. They reasoned that our spherical world and the human eye are shaped similarly. Both are liquid pools. Our eyes see light reflected off physical objects. The light bounces off these objects and reaches our eyes. We see these light images upside down with our eyes; and our brain flips the light images right-side up for us. So it is with the world. The sorcerer therefore looks up at the sky and recognizes that light could bounce off the atmospheric ceiling of this sphere we call the world. And since the atmospheric ceiling to our world is curved to conform to the shape of the world, the light bounces down in a distorted fashion the way you might see things in those bent mirrors at the carnival.

But with our limited eyes, do we really see beyond the ceiling to our world, or just the light bounced off the ceiling? For that matter, do we ever really see anything accurately? Not directly. What we see is light bounced off other physical objects. Of course, light quality varies. Also, light doesn't make ninety-degree turns, as a rule. So something just around the bend or beyond the horizon is beyond our range of vision, as a general rule. In a sense, too, it's outside our moving reality, since it isn't part of our integrated world of experience. (The most frightening thing, perhaps, is that we can't even look into our own faces directly, but must trust mirror images of how we assume we look.)

In the spirit of the sorcerer's explanation, it's easy to see how the eyes can be confused and the seer can become disoriented. If we consider again the Yacqui's world ceiling, we see that the light that bounces off the Earth's atmosphere and back down to our eyes on the ground could just as easily come from the ground below as the stratosphere above. Consequently, we could be looking up at the heavens and seeing reflections of ourselves projected from the ground below. Well, most cosmologies and most religions are decidedly made by people anyway, as we tend to craft god and godliness in our own image, only a little grander in scale.

From a more scientific approach, we see modern wizards of physics grappling with some of the same basic questions today. Another group of physicists recently determined the likely existence of extra dimensions wrapped in circles so tiny that we have not detected them. They also believe there could be extra dimensions as large as a millimeter that we cannot detect. Modern string theories, in seeking to explain the composition of the known universe, have dusted off the 1920s research of Swedish physicist Oskar Klein and Polish mathematician Theodor Kaluza, and their unified theory of gravity and electromagnetism that required an extra dimension. For our elaborate, present string theories to work with mathematical consistency, modern physicists say that no fewer than ten spatial dimensions are required. (These extra dimensions, however, can only be detected through gravity. Consequently, researchers are now seeking to upgrade our somewhat limited understanding of gravity.)

Clearly, we live in a physical universe with boundaries, limited by our perception to see beyond these boundaries. There may be an entirely different universe out there, just beyond our physical grasp and just out of eyeshot. A physical journey cannot take you there, nor can you spot it in a telescope.

We cannot imagine more than the three dimensions of our universe, Ouspensky lamented. As linear thinkers trapped in a linear world, we cannot construct more than three independent perpendiculars, he said. Consequently, we are forced to admit the fact of the limitedness of our space in relation to geometric possibilities. Ouspensky was quick to add, however, that the limitation might lie within ourselves, if the properties of space are created by some limitation of consciousness.

Indeed, Ouspensky was one of the first researchers in this area of study to suggest that higher consciousness was the one and only legitimate way to explore and experience this non-ordinary reality. The meditator, in a state of heightened awareness, engages the higher mind and leaves his body and the limitations of this physical universe behind. The person in heightened consciousness is not restricted by the physical laws of this visible universe, but can explore beyond the senses. He can also explore beyond normal perception and beyond any cultural frame of reference. Ouspensky agreed that consciousness can separate from the body and operate outside a material framework. All serious physicists seem to concur that the important function of consciousness cannot be ignored in our attempts to explore the limits of reality.

Therefore, the boundaries to our known universe are not limitations at all to the higher mind and the meditator who seeks to explore alternate reality in the non-ordinary world. In fact, the verification of alternate realities in alternate universes with additional dimensions makes the possible adventure even more exciting to the soul traveler. Alternate realities do exist—just beyond our physical reach, but accessible through heightened consciousness.

Would you like to explore a sense of higher-dimensional reality in this physical world, without entering higher consciousness? Scientists Dimopoulos, Dvali, and Arkani-Hamed suggest that a simple game of pocket billiards or pool could give you some idea of the sort of conditions that might lead to experiencing a higher-dimensional reality. At least it will give you the concept of what conditions could create the possibility of experiencing higher dimensions. Think of the billiard balls moving across the surface of the table as particles like protons and electrons. As far as our billiard balls are concerned, the universe of the billiard table is two-dimensional. When one ball strikes another hard, they can produce sound waves that travel in three dimensions. This action carries energy from the surface of the table. The resulting travel of the sound waves of our striking billiard balls is similar to gravitons, which can travel in full, high-dimensional space.

You can set up a pool table with balls in a personal exercise to give you some idea how this might work. Of course, only exacting study of the motion of the billiard balls could determine the energy that is carried from the table's surface into higher dimensions.

Billiard Table Exercise

You'll need:
- Pool or billiard table
- Billiard balls
- Pool cue

Directions

Line up a shot with your pool cue or stick. Using the cue stick, shoot the white cue ball into another ball on the table, striking it hard. Note the sound of the balls crashing into each other and the way the balls bounce wildly toward the edge of the table after they collide. Consider the sound energy created and the way the balls attempt to leave the playing surface. Only the cushions on the sides of the table prevent them from leaving the playing surface.

You might experiment with other shots with the balls, perhaps with top spin on the white cue ball to force the cue ball to jump up with striking the object ball, perhaps hopping off the table.

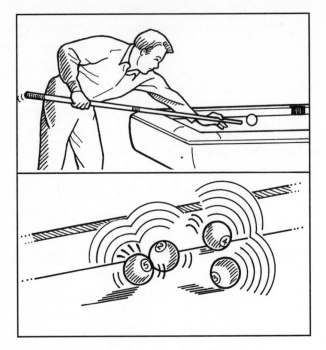

Figure 4 • BILLIARD TABLE EXERCISE

Another variation could be to hit the white cue ball with underspin (draw) or side spin (English) to make the balls more active upon contact. You are creating sound energy and direction with your shots.

Consider how your table surface is a relatively confined area, unless the balls wildly jump the banks of the table after impact, leaving the realm of the billiard table and the limited dimensions of the pool game behind.

CHAPTER 8

Riding carefully selected time waves

HAVE YOU EVER noticed how opportunities seem to drift your way at certain times like big waves that suddenly wash ashore? If you were a surfer, you might wait all day to find the right wave to ride—that incredibly big one with all of the power behind it. You would watch the tide and wait for the right timing. You would notice the regular wave action, but then observe how every so often a really huge wave would come along. That's the opportunity you seek. You get ready for that big wave and then hop onboard for a big ride when it does finally come your way. Watching for the right wave and getting onboard on time is the trick to the surfer's success.

That's true of opportunists in any walk of life. They watch for the right wave to come along and then climb aboard when it passes by at full crest with enough power to take you where you want to go. Not every moment holds the same opportunities, of course. Picking the right time is crucial.

There is an optimum time for just about everything, if you watch patiently and ready yourself for the opportunity. It depends on the sort of wave you want to catch and where you want to go. You can't really expect nature to freely give you a specific opportunity whenever you want it. Nature always extends opportunities, but not always in the order we might desire. Consequently, we need to get into synch with nature and determine her rhythm of life. This creates a certain harmonic balance and also improves your sense of timing for the natural opportunities that arise periodically in nature. If you were to stay at the beach long enough with the surfers, you would notice that tides change periodically, and longer waves—while not frequent—do appear now and again with a certain pattern. Once again, the trick to catching them involves careful observation and patience.

Being present when the big wave or opportunity appears is only half the trick, however. What you do with the opportunity is the other half of the trick. Surf riders, for instance, want to catch the wave at the right time. They want to catch the wave when it's on the rise and beginning to reach its full size and power. They do not want to catch the wave when it's already on the decline. Also, if they catch the wave at its peak when it begins to crest, it will likely bowl them over with its brute force. So they prefer to catch the big wave on its way up and not on its way down.

That's true in many situations. In business, people often talk about catching opportunities as they are forming and having the right sense of time. When stock value is climbing, investors want to buy into a company before its market price reaches a high-water mark. Naturally, when the stock price begins a steady decline, many wise investors will jump off that wave and find another on the rise.

In marketing, business-savvy people want to catch a trend just before it reaches popularity to ride the wave of public interest all the way to the bank. Johnny-come-lately marketers who try to cash in on a trend when it's at the peak of popularity often find that they are gearing up too late, and then end up with a warehouse full of unmarketable hoops or gizmos. The trick is to get in there early when the wave is beginning to form, and ride it as far as it will take you. Then there's always another big wave to catch if you are willing to wait for it.

Gold rush prospectors who stayed too long at played-out strike sites went bust in California and Alaska with the false impression that the good fortune of the original strikes would prove endless. It's the classic problem of not being in the right place at the right time. Obviously, a person needs to keep both eyes and ears open to changing conditions and be willing to move around to find new, golden opportunities. Once again, timing is everything.

It's been said many times as a bit of folk wisdom that lightning won't strike twice in the same spot. That may be true. Also, it may be false. It all depends on where you are standing in anticipation. If you are standing atop the Empire State Building, you might get struck by lightning several times a year. It's a fact that the spire of the famous New York skyscraper does attract lightning bolts. If you stand inside a metal church steeple that resembles a giant lightning rod, you could encounter frequent electrical storm damage, as well. So don't think that ringing church bells could necessarily keep you out of harm's way. You need to remain observant and be ready to adapt successfully to changing conditions around you. Opportunities, like lightning bolts, are all around us. They rain down from the heavens. The problem is perceiving them and having enough personal power to pluck the right one at the right time to use properly.

The Tai Chi dancer moves within a defined and observed field of energy all around her. She dances with the energy in nature. Perhaps we shouldn't think of energy as a force without a face, but as a dance partner with personality. The Tai Chi dancer responds to the forms of energy around her and blends with those forms. She adds the energy forms to her own form and becomes one with nature and one with the moment. Together they make a dance, and that dance is the rhythm of life at that moment and in that expression.

I have witnessed the extent to which Tai Chi masters can gather energy around them at a moment's notice and employ it. Once when I was leading workshops in Kirlian photography at the Total Living Center in Sioux Falls, South Dakota, one of the students who had studied Tai Chi surprised me with a demonstration. Since the workshop was about gathering photographic proof of energy, this woman thought that I would especially appreciate her little energy demonstration. During a break in the day, she invited me to a quiet room apart from the others and closed the door. She said that she wanted to show me something really amazing, which related to our study of harnessed energy around us. She walked to the far side of the room and faced me. She pulled a metal apparatus out of her purse and set the purse down. The apparatus was actually a pair of angle irons on a swivel. Extending the angle irons in front of her, she walked toward me. I wondered for a moment whether she was divining for water below us. My questions were soon answered. She got close to me and then stopped, with the angle irons extended out toward me.

"Watch the rods," she instructed. Suddenly, the angle irons swiveled forward and closed like a gate, or barricade, before me.

"Try to walk toward me," she said.

I tried walking toward her, but found that I couldn't. I can't really explain it. But the truth of the matter is that I was stopped from advancing by an invisible force.

She looked at me and smiled.

"Okay," she said. "Now we'll try something different. Wait just a minute."

I watched the rods in her hands and noticed that they were starting to spin backward.

"There," she said. "Now try to remain where you are and don't move."

When the rods started to swivel in another direction, however, it felt as though they were pulling me like magnets toward them.

Try as I would, I just couldn't stay still. I felt my body moving forward against my will. I was reminded of those old horror movies in

which Count Dracula calls his victim forward, and the victim is pow-
erless to refuse. It feels very strange when the body lumbers forward
involuntarily. The movements are rather spasmodic and not well
coordinated.

"This is Tai Chi, isn't it?" I asked.

She nodded. Then she put her rods away and released me. What a
strange feeling it is to be held by an invisible force and then suddenly
and mysteriously find yourself free from that force again. The
woman and I returned to the class where we continued to discuss
the topic of the day: how energy is all around us and can be tapped,
if we are perceptive. Her quick demonstration of the magic formula
conceive, perceive, achieve, and believe made me speak with greater con-
viction than ever before. Indeed, opportunity is all around us and
energized to help us.

When I reflect on the Tai Chi woman dancing with the energy
around her, I am stuck by the personality and cooperation of energy
for the person fortunate to engage it. Certainly some people seem
better at charming invisible forces around them and engaging their
help than others. All of us, however, have this potential, as we are all
exposed to the same forces of nature that surround us. Helena
Blavatskly suggested in *The Voice of the Silence* that we serve Nature,
and if we do, that she would serve us. It's easy to see the potential
for assistance in that statement, and also the personality of natural
forces around us.

The invisible forces that psychic and author Louis Gittner channels
describe themselves as a collection of energy gathered together at a
specific time and place to help and provide answers. Gittner has chan-
neled their explanations about the nature of creation and human des-
tiny faithfully for years. They descend upon his chest as he reclines on
his back in a sleeping prophet position to enter a meditative state. A
witness to the event sees a gathering of light upon Gittner's chest,
even though the room where he reclines may be dark-proofed with
curtains drawn and lights extinguished. The collection of lights upon
his chest resemble the darting flecks of light that my son and I saw in

the rustic log cabin behind the Outlook Inn. Certainly, energy does appear to be a collection of entities with personality and a willingness to help those with enough personal power to perceive them and engage them.

Another author, Genevieve Paulson, works with students in workshops in this general area. She is the author of *Kundalini and the Chakras and Energy Focused Meditation*. With her son, Stephen Paulson, she's also written the amazing book *Reincarnation*. Together they have led workshops on time waves. They see time as radiating toward our world like rays or waves. There are different kinds of time waves— some longer and some shorter. Some have different properties. It's almost as though you could ride the right time wave, if you could find it and grab it.

You could live your life trying to select the right time waves for every situation, as you go through each day. My own lifestyle is an example of this approach. Sure, I prepare short-term goals, intermediate goals, and even long-term goals. I think them through carefully, internalize them, write them down, and determine what is required to bring them to fruition. I realize, for instance, that I may need help to accomplish my goals, either in the form of assistance from other people or circumstances that need to be correctly aligned. I realize that I need to charge myself with the responsibility for becoming an agent of change. Then I need to work out all of the steps required to bring my goals into being. I need to visualize the goal becoming realized, and even the steps toward achieving the goal. I will even employ the Gittner magic formula for altering my personal reality: *conceive-perceive-achieve-believe.*

I even plan my days and weeks with somewhat detailed to-do lists. These are activities that I hope to accomplish in a more or less descending order of importance. Where I break with the gurus of day planners, I suppose, is over the timing of my daily and weekly goals. I refuse to force myself to commit to a very specific time of day when I will accomplish any task. For people who have worked with time management systems or day planners and had to plan out their daily and weekly activities by the time of day, this might seem a little odd. The whole point behind these workbook systems, of course, is to make an appointment with yourself to do something at a specific time of day. Most of these day planners want you to commit to a precise time within fifteen or thirty minutes and stick to that plan no matter what.

I refuse to do that for a very good reason. The timing might be wrong. Sometimes you can just sense that the timing is wrong. I don't mean that you can't drive to town at 5 P.M. via the interstate or can't do your grocery shopping between 6 P.M. and 7 P.M., for instance. You can go ahead and follow such a preordained schedule. The question of the moment, however, is whether that's the best use of the time immediately available to you. Does it feel right to go shopping at 6 P.M., or do you feel that something else would work better at that time? You can only determine this on the spot, when the time comes. It's a little like sizing up the waves on the ocean. There's a pattern to the way things come your way, but you need to watch very carefully for the big wave that comes only every so often.

To size up the situation, you need to slow down everything around you in your mind's eye and control your sensory perception. You need to survey the theatre of moving reality in front of you and all around you. You will begin to access the situations you have been given. If you are a baseball runner who wants to steal second base, for instance, you might stop down all the action in your head and stop the surrounding sensory irritations that might distract you. This might mean internally controlling crowd noise, confusing blurs of other activity, odd smells, and the aching feeling of your sore feet on the ground. You need to focus. You have been given some useful information and helpful circumstances. You focus on these things. You observe that the pitcher and catcher are not aware of your intent to steal second base, and are not watching you. You notice that they are moving slowly and look preoccupied with their own thoughts, not wary of activity in the infield where you are planning your theft. You notice that the second baseman is straying far from the bag and not anticipating any theft on your part. You observe that the ground is in good shape and offers a fast track for your sprint to second base, should you try to steal a base. These are the givens of the situation. They are physical certainties for the most part. You can weigh them in your focused assessment of your chances to achieve your goal.

Then you consider if the timing is right. This is not a physical reading you can access in the same way. It's a little more like taking a wind reading to see which way the wind is blowing. Determining the best timing for a situation is an intangible. You will need to put your feelers out. To do this, you must alter your consciousness momentarily and enter a different state. If you stop the world in the sense that you turn off sensory perception and make everything slow down in your mind's eye for only a split second, you can enter a meditative state where answers are available to you. You can enter this altered state of consciousness quickly with practice, as we have seen. You can exit it just as quickly, with practice. You can enter and exit this state of higher consciousness any time you desire, with experience and focused attention. You don't need to assume a perfect lotus position or hum a mantra. The warrior athlete is disciplined to control the world around him, and enter the world of spirit at a moment's notice to retrieve needed insight.

So we see our first-base runner about to steal second. He assesses the situation and determines what given circumstances help or hinder his goal to steal a base. He tunes out distracting sensory perception, slows down the world for a split second, and enters a heightened state of attention. In slowing down the world, his momentary departure into heightened awareness takes very little time at all. In that state of heightened awareness, he assesses whether the time is right for him to steal the base. This is not simply a determination of whether he can run fast enough or outmaneuver his opponents. It's a reading on the strength and quality of the energy surrounding him. Sometimes, as we have seen, there seems to be all the time in the world to accomplish some feat. At other times, there's seems to be little or no time at all. Time varies from situation to situation.

I can explain how I handle events of the day in my day planner. I might have four or five things scheduled for the morning in descending order of importance. When I am ready to tackle any of these goals at the time I expected to approach them, however, I step back and assess the situation to take a time reading. I take a quick reading to momentarily enter a state of heightened awareness. With practice, I have learned to pop in and out of this state very quickly. I must confess that I once had trouble popping into this state carelessly at almost any time, because it feels so good. Now I plan my little departures into this state.

In this state of heightened awareness, you can read the invisible world around you. This is the world of energy, spirit, and time. It is an elastic world. In this world, things can stretch long or contract short. It's a world outside of physical restrictions.

When I take a reading of a situation, I want to know if there is enough energy around me to accomplish what I have in mind. I want to know the quality of the time around me. Does it feel like the sort of time for the goal I have in mind at the moment? If not, I consider the other activities I have planned for the same morning. I take a reading on these other activities to see if the time feels right for any of them at the moment. Then I go with the feeling. Always trust your instinct. Never doubt what you bring from the spirit world in your meditations. They call it heightened awareness, because your awareness is raised in that state. Do not doubt that, or else the magical formula *conceive-perceive-achieve-believe* is broken. Then your reality base is broken.

I never doubt my readings when I assess the timing for a situation. If it feels like I shouldn't be at a certain place, or doing a certain thing at that specific time, then I postpone that activity. I perceive that there isn't the quality of time energy to support that activity most successfully. I make apologies to friends sometimes for these post-ponements and attempt to reschedule. I try to avoid forcing the issue. You can't force nature; you can only work harmoniously with her, or suffer the possible consequences.

Here's a simple, but telling, exercise you can try.

"Catching the Wave" Exercise

You'll need:

- An ocean beach
- To put yourself on the shore, facing out to the ocean
- To make certain that the tide is an incoming tide (consult a newspaper or a tide book, available at sports stores)
- To be sure that you have enough light to watch the waves carefully

Directions

Watch the waves of the ocean as they strike the shore in front of you during an incoming tide. Get a sense of timing for the pattern of the waves. Note the pattern for larger waves that hit the beach. Feel the power of the waves. Feel the energy of the waves. Sense the timing. There is a pattern to nature. Timing is everything. Develop a keen sense of timing with regard to nature and nature's energy.

Alternate Exercise – "Catching the Wind"

If you do not live close to a beach with an incoming tide, then stand outside facing the wind on a windy day. Get a sense of timing for the gusts of wind that strike you. Note the pattern for the larger gusts of wind that pass through every so often. Feel the power of the wind. Feel the energy of the wind. Sense the timing of the gusts. Recognize the patterns in nature. Attempt to acquire a sense of timing with regard to nature's energy.

CHAPTER 9

Becoming totally awake and alert

MOST OF US just go through the basic motions of living out each day in a repetitive pattern of behavior. It's work, eat, and sleep, followed by more work, eat, and sleep. Once in a while, something interrupts us or catches our fancy; and we are diverted momentarily. Then we get back to our "work-eat-sleep" cycle. Sound familiar? To many people, sadly, this is a familiar pattern of living. But is this really living? These people don't get involved. They do not see much of what is happening around them. They do not play a part. They live like the monkeys that hear no evil, see no evil, and speak no evil. For that matter, they hear, see, and speak little or nothing at all. They are tuned out to life. After all, people who see and hear what evil is going on around them are held somewhat responsible to step up to the problem and get involved. People oblivious to what goes on around them, on the other hand, are not expected to play hero or do anything remotely heroic or noble.

They also miss out on everything else that life has to offer, of course. You have to pity all of those people who walk through town or through the park with earplugs jammed up their ears. They might be listening to their favorite tunes over and over and feeling good in their own little comfort zones; but they're missing out on everything around them. It's hard to hear the robins sing with earplugs. It's hard to hear a helpful warning. It's hard to hear a call for help. It's hard to receive any new information, as they walk through the day with earplugs jammed up their ears. Life, after all, is experiential and not a canned performance.

Sometimes I think we have really lost something with our technological advancement as a species. We lost our animal alertness to the world around us. We are fast losing our sense of wonder and curiosity about the world. Now that we believe we have mastered our environment to our simplistic satisfaction, we have isolated ourselves from the world and decided to take a nice, long, comfortable nap. A tree could fall in the forest, and nobody would hear it. Most of us have left the woods behind. We have left nature behind. Indeed, we have left all of the world behind except for our climate-controlled, gated homes where we curl up with our electronic toys in our recliners.

As a working journalist on a newspaper, I always tried to stay alert to the world around me. That's more than just keeping up on the world events we call news. It's seeing, hearing, and feeling the greater world around you. It's developing a keen sense of observation and a sense of empathy for the sacredness of all life around us. I recall how I would test my skills of observation throughout the day by trying to absorb as many details of each passing scene as I could. The trick is not only to see, hear, and feel as much as possible, but to internalize the information in a way that is meaningful. That way, you develop a connection to the world in which you live. That includes the rocks, trees, and bugs. My tests of observation wouldn't be complete until I could recall as much as possible of the scene I had just witnessed. When I thought that I had a good, general grasp of the countryside including how the brush looked and where the boulders lay, then I would grade my attempts at total observation when I passed that way the next time.

Try as hard as I could, I would always get something wrong. Of course, that's largely due to the fact that the world changes around us constantly and never stays stagnant. In time, everything changes. The birds migrate. The weather changes the way that nature looks from season to season. Likewise, the characters in every scene you witness move around from time to time. That's the way it is with life. It keeps changing. Consequently, our knowledge and under-standing of the world around us become outdated very quickly. We must remain alert and fully conscious of the constant changes of the world around us.

Wild animals, by contrast, are very alert to the changing world around them. Not coincidentally, they also have better survival skills than most people. The house cat and lap dog we consider so totally depend on us would probably survive much better wandering in the woods than we would, if calamity ever put all of us out of our homes. All animals, with the sole exception of people, seem able to relate to nature and read her signs enough to coexist in the wild. They sense a coming storm. They smell water. They know where to find shelter and food. They do not panic when they are alone in nature, because they realize that they are not really alone. The rain, trees, and sun are their friends. By contrast, we fear nature as a species, for the most part. Many people are afraid to get out of their cars on a weekend outing. We distrust and fear other animals basically.

The irony to all of this is that we've learned most of what we know from other animals. Birds, really, taught us how to fly and inspired us to try, despite our lack of wings. Dolphins taught us how to swim and showed us that the water can be safe, despite our lack of aquatic gills. We see in other animals, such as the wolf or horse (pack animals, just like us) the models for good mothering and patient rear-ing of children. Our best athletes still emulate the big cats for their power, speed, and agility afoot. Athletes and fans of athletics like to name their teams after animals, making them sort of modern totems for the tribes of people today who admire the speed of the falcon and eagle, the daring of the colt and ram, and the power of the bronco and bear.

These wild animals live totally in the moment, without tortuous worries about the past or the future. They are confident that nature will provide for them, despite the fact they have next to nothing by our standards. They have their eyes, their ears, and their alert consciousness to everything that is happening around them at that exact moment in time. They respond accordingly.

I remember the director of Pet Rescue in Illinois explaining to me how the abused, neglected, and forgotten dogs and cats in her shelter could nonetheless extend love and hope unconditionally to total strangers who would encounter them locked in their cages.

"They are more noble than we are," she would tell me. "No matter what they have lived through, they can put all that aside and reach out again. We could learn a lot from them."

It's true. They hold no grudges for the most part. They have no big, private agenda for how they want things to be in the future. They live totally in the moment and can turn their lives around at any moment.

If only we could live totally in the moment, as they do. Surely, that's something we can do, if every other animal on earth seems able to do it. And yet we see only the greatest masters able to do it consistently. Author Alan Watts, who wrote *The Way of Zen,* urged his students to simply be in the moment. The greatest things could happen to you and you could realize great insights by simply taking this one step, he promised. Certainly, the great mysteries of the ages and hidden truth are only revealed to those few people who can adjust their consciousness to receive the information. Any communication requires a clear signal to carry the message and a tuned-in receiver. Watts wanted his students to be that receiver and find that clear signal.

But the mystic also sought a proper teacher from the Eastern mystery schools to come to the West and guide his young Zen meditators. He predicted such a person would appear and prepared the masses. Ironically, perhaps, Watts himself became that guru. He was a college professor from American who saw where he wanted his students to go and a fair idea even as a novice to Zen as to how to get there. It was truly a case of the message being more important than the credentials of the messenger. It also reminds us that a hero is somebody who perceives responsibility and simply steps up to the plate to take appropriate action in a selfless, loving manner.

Perhaps that is what true heroism is all about, as the Bhagavad Gita of India suggests in charting a responsible warrior's concern over the consequences of taking right action in the face of mounting karmic debt. It requires courage, responsibility, and sober discernment to determine right action and take it for the good of the whole without petty concern for oneself. Krishnamurti's little booklet *At the Feet of the Master* (under the pen name Alcyone) encourages spiritually evolving people to hold selfless action and focused discernment in high regard as they select their way on the path of life.

You, too, can become a hero in your own theatre of reality, if you live in the moment broadly and fill the moment with your conscious presence. It's a bit like starring in your own movie. Obviously, this starring role requires active participation and interaction, not just passive meditation. Many people think that meditation is simply sitting quietly in a restful state. Nothing could be further from the truth. True meditation is active participation, not passive introspection. That is why I refer to being in the moment in this context as living broadly in the moment and filling the moment with your presence.

You can reach this state of heightened awareness in a moment while you are washing dishes or even throwing out the trash, if you do it right. You can reach this state of higher consciousness while walking the dog or waiting on a street corner for a bus. The place or circumstances is not particularly limiting. What you must bring to the circumstance is a perfect sense of timing by fully seizing the moment. You do this with your total consciousness. This is not simply a mental exercise in which you concentrate intensely. You must be fully involved with every cell of your body. You must sense the moment with every fiber of your being.

Krishnamurti told a story once about gentlemen he had known in India who had trouble meditating at their designated hour of the day, because children outside their meditation room were too noisy. He pointed out that the children shouldn't be told not to laugh and sing to keep things quiet, but that true meditators should be able to reach a state of heightened consciousness in any situation by personally tuning out distracting noise around them.

Tuning out the world's distractions to reach a state of higher consciousness is like simple subtraction. You strip away the nonessentials in your life and through simple elimination eventually get down to only the things that are important at the moment. The final formula reads $1 - 0 = 1$. The end number should be 1. You and the world of higher consciousness are one. In this altered state, you see that all are one. In this state of higher awareness, everything reaches harmonic resonance without the dissonance of noise and without clashes. You see the interconnectedness of all life and how all of life is sacred and precious. You see that all of creation is one and made essentially from the same substances, with splendid variation of patterning to make life more colorful and interesting. In this state of heightened awareness, you may experience life fully in a moment's time.

A Zen master in this state can see a tree and become the tree for the moment. He can experience the tree and know just how the tree feels and thinks. He can feel the wind rustling through the tree and sense the tall grandeur of its magnificent branches to the sky. This is because the Zen master reduces the distance between himself and the tree. He and the tree become one, joined in consciousness. This is a joining that can never really occur in the physical sense, but only in a state of heightened consciousness.

This sense of oneness can happen anywhere and anytime, if you prepare for it. Surely shamans have experienced this on countless occasions in their states of altered consciousness, as they become one with the bear or become one with the eagle to bring back to their peoples the visions of their journeys into the spirit world.

I experienced this personally for the first time when I lived in southeastern Alaska in the 1970s and worked for the *Ketchikan Daily News*. It was on a weekend outing above Harriet Lake. A friend had encouraged me to go deer hunting with him that winter. Now, I don't hunt (or fish) any longer. That was a long time ago for me; and I have made many life-altering changes in my outlook since those days. Even then, I was reluctant to go hunting, but in the end agreed with the belief that we would not actually confront any deer or see any action other than a nice day of hiking around in nature. I figured that I could use the rifle scope in my borrowed weapon as a tele-scope to survey the beautiful Alaskan landscape dusted with the first, wondrous snow of winter.

I remember walking across the frozen lake gingerly in our heavy winter clothing. I could hear the ice creaking beneath my heavy boots in places on the lake. It was a perfectly clear and quiet day as we walked across the lake—a splendid winter's morning. I could hear a variety of birds making their calls and could identify some of them, including the screech of the big ravens. But what were the say-ing? Beware, here comes a man?

My friend and I climbed up a muddy embankment on the other side of the lake that was frozen in places and slippery in other spots. At the top of the embankment, we were exhausted from the climb and a little lightheaded. We stopped to catch our breath. At the top of the hill, I surveyed the lake behind us and a meadow in front of us. I was struck by the awesome beauty of the rustic setting. I don't think that I had ever before witnessed such breathtaking beauty in nature.

The combination of the exhausting climb and mood-altering beauty of nature seemed to have their effect on me. As my eyes took in the sights around me and I smelled the rare, clear area of the Alaskan hillside, I realized that this was nothing I had ever experi-enced before. Suddenly, all of the noise inside my head began to clear away, and I felt a quiet peacefulness. I became alertly aware of the still majesty of the moment and the way the morning light cast its incredible shadows upon the snow on the meadow before me. The meadow was like a cathedral of trees. Even the ravens on the tall evergreen treetops at the far side of the field fluttered from limb to limb silently. As I looked down the mountain to the right of the meadow, I could the blue Alaskan waters and outer islands in the distance. Everything in this quiet cathedral of trees seemed to be happening in slow motion, as though frozen magically in time.

I felt myself beginning to enter an altered state with a shift in my total consciousness. I was dumbstruck by what I saw and felt in this magical meadow. I felt a harmonic resonance with my surroundings such that I had never felt before. I do not know exactly how long I stood there in the snow at one side of the meadow, just watching and absorbing it all. I felt a part of the meadow, not an intruder. Like the still trees, I just stood there like a statue, transfixed in time.

Suddenly, something caught my eye. A deer had bolted into the meadow. It stood almost in the middle of the meadow and turned its head toward me. It had an elegant set of antlers on its head. Slowly, I lifted the scope of the rifle to my eye for a better look. I looked through the peephole of the scope and directly into the eye of the deer. It looked directly at me with kind, curious eyes. I looked deeper into its eyes. The deer continued to gaze directly at me, without twitching or even blinking. I felt myself going deeper and deeper into the eyes of the deer.

Then something quite unusual happened. I felt that I was looking back at a man pointing at me from the far side of the meadow. I was looking back at myself through the eyes of the deer! I felt snow falling on my deer hide. I felt the heavy weight of the rack of antlers on my head. I saw my warm breath rising in the cold air from my snout. Then I looked back at the man pointing at me from the far side of the meadow.

Suddenly I was back in my body, holding the rifle. I blinked my eyes and began to twitch. I became aware that I was pointing a loaded weapon at the deer. My biggest concern became the safety and well-being of that deer. My imagination quickly engaged and began to race through various solutions. I could lower the rifle, I thought. But then I wondered whether I should do it quickly, the way my instinct of fear told me to do. If I did it with a jerking motion, however, I might accidentally discharge the weapon. On the other hand, if I lowered it slowly, the deer was exposed to a possible discharge for a longer period of danger. I quickly wanted to put this poor deer out of harm's way and felt the greatest guilt for putting this innocent creature in such a position—here in its own personal sanctuary.

Then I considered simply reaching up to the safety lock with my trigger finger to engage the safety mechanism. That way, the gun could never fire accidentally. As I slowly lowered the rifle tip to the ground, I snapped on the safety lock. Then I looked up to see the deer again. It had disappeared before my very eyes. I could see it nowhere.

I removed all rounds of ammunition from the rifle and put them into my coat pocket. With the rifle pointed safety to the ground, I began my solo trek down the muddy incline to the lake. Strangely, I had few thoughts as I walked back across the lake. I remember the ice beginning to crack in the middle. Even that didn't faze me. I simply moved closer to one shore and took the long walk around the lake, walking on the water.

When I reached the truck at the other end of the lake, I put the rifle away immediately. I would never hunt again. I knew now that life was far too sacred and precious to be taken away. I also knew now that all life is connected and related and that I could no longer separate myself from the rest of the world in the way I once had. I had personal experience as evidence of that.

I began to think about the deer again and wondered whether I should try to feel sorry for him in his rough surroundings. No, I decided. After all, he had a sense of peace and harmony with his surroundings that I envied. Then I wondered whether I should feel sorry for my hunting companion who in his blind enthusiasm was still stalking the mountain meadows for something to kill. No, I was happy in the thought that he would one day discover what I had discovered and put down his rifle, too. In fact, I was his biggest fan in rooting for him to reach this discovery. I decided that it would come to him when the time was right.

Years later when I worked for a newspaper in Oregon, I interviewed a neighbor on Mt. Hood who had a personal encounter with a tree in the same way I had joined with the deer in the meadow. This man wrote children's stories. In fact, that was the reason I interviewed him—because he wrote children's stories. I did not know at first that he had any special rapport with a tree. In the course of the interview, I asked him why he always gave credit to someone named Omarr in the front of his children's books. His answer was pretty startling. He said that Omarr was his friend and collaborator and that I should meet him myself. He walked me to the side of his house and sat on an old stump.

"This is Omarr," he told me, pointing down to the stump below him.

He said that one day when he sat on the stump, it started to tell him a children's story. The stump even introduced himself as Omarr, the tree. For years, the stump and the man continued their close collaboration, sharing personal thoughts and ideas.

Many people, it seems, have similar stories about joining with trees. My son and his best friend lay beneath heavy forest canopy with me in Brightwood, Oregon, one summer afternoon. We all closed our eyes to try to communicate with the old-growth, giant trees towering above us. It was a dark, little clearing in the woods with huge trees crowded together and blocking out most of the light. We lay down in a patch of light that peeked through the trees. I had no idea whether we'd be successful, but knew from my encounter with the deer in the meadow that such meetings were possible under the right conditions.

After a short while, my body grew numb and my hearing dimmed. I felt that I was entering a state of higher consciousness and only hoped that my thoughts would reach the trees so that we could communicate. I really had no idea how to talk to a tree or how it might talk back. I started to feel the hairs on the back of my head tingle. My eyes were closed, yet I was superalert. I thought I heard a small voice that sounded something like a little child.

"Want to know a secret?" it asked. "I don't mind the bugs that eat my leaves. If they didn't eat my leaves at the top, the sunlight couldn't reach the small trees below me."

I bolted up and popped open my eyes.

"Did you hear anything?" I asked the two boys.

My son's friend smiled.

"I did," he said. "Did you?"

"Yes," I answered. "But you tell me what you heard first."

"I think a tree talked to me," he said. "It was saying something funny about bugs or something."

"Did he say anything about light?" I challenged.

"Yeah. Something about how trees need light to grow."

We walked back up the road to our houses near the trees in silence, stunned by what we had heard. The tree's message rocked us both, and we started to talk about it. The neighbor boy said he was amazed that the tree had spoken to him and chosen to discuss something that interested them both—bugs. Personally speaking, I was impressed in another way. I was moved that the tree seemed so aware of all life around it and wanted to share the sunlight at some expense to itself. That's the foremost thing it wanted us to know. I'd like to become as totally aware as that tree.

Krishnamurti spoke and wrote often about his concern that most people were asleep in spirit and sleepwalking through life in this unfortunate condition. It was his prediction, however, that our world soon would experience a great awakening when the sleeping masses would become fully conscious. This is what becoming awake and alert meant to Krishnamurti—spiritual beings rising to higher consciousness. Isn't it odd that most people haven't been able to achieve what a tree or even a stump can do most naturally?

Tree Exercise

You'll need:
- To find a tree in a somewhat secluded or private spot outdoors
- You might want a beach blanket or something large enough for you to use as ground cover in laying down on the dirt or grass next to the tree

Directions

Lie down on your back next to the tree with your head facing the sky. I would suggest that you do this during sunlight with the light brightly shining upon you.

Close your eyes tightly and concentrate on the colors you are able to see, even with your eyes closed.

Clear your mind of any internal dialogue or thoughts and become oblivious to any distracting sounds or activities around you.

Allow your body to become numb and enter a state of heightened consciousness.

Think only of the tree beside you. Feel the tree. Sense the tree. Without words, reach out to the tree. Make a connection. Become one with the tree.

Wait patiently. Remember, there is no normal sense of time in this state of heightened awareness. Allow yourself to drift in this time-lessness, becoming one with the tree.

Be alert. Your impressions could be a feeling, a mood, a thought, or simple statement. This is an exercise in attentive listening.

Acknowledge what you hear or perceive. Do not dismiss it or doubt it. Trust what you perceive. Thank the tree.

CHAPTER 10

Stretching time

whenever it suits you

YOU CAN STRETCH time whenever it suits you. After all, time is elastic and something you can control. We must remember that people invented time as a measuring device for human convenience. Outside of our experience—as in the world of nature, for instance—time doesn't exist in the way we know it. It's really just a matter of human perception. Therefore, you can control time on a personal level through your perception. If you need a situation to last longer, you can adjust your perception of an event or situation, so that time seems to you to last forever. If you need time to pass quickly, you can also shorten it through manipulation of your perceptive reality.

Remember that the only real time in creation is the actual duration or how long something takes to happen. If you are the agent of change, then you can determine the duration involved. The wonderful thing about human beings, of course, is that we are potential agents of change. We have wills. That is, we can will things to happen or not happen. We can exercise our wills. We can exert our will power. Furthermore, we can transform energy into action. We are dynamos, really.

Nothing can happen without an agent of change. Nothing can happen without a desire to change. All of creation is in perpetual motion, moving toward change. But there must be a desire, a will, or an agent of change to act as that dynamo of change.

What changes would you make? Your potential is virtually unlimited, restricted only by your imagination, perhaps. Noted author Dr. Michael Newton, in his groundbreaking book *Journey of Souls,* describes the creation work that people do in their lives between lives. His work is based upon years of careful research in case studies of clinical patients placed under deepest hypnosis. Under hypnosis, people began to remember their lives between lives. It was simply a matter of asking the right questions and establishing a pattern of response. Dr. Newton found that some people remember a time between their earthly lives when they returned to a place to regroup with their soul families as light beings. Apparently, these are times to reflect on the challenges and goals of living a physical existence and a chance to discuss your progress in spiritual evolution with your cluster group of souls and your group's leader, who are with you through many lifetimes. Remarkably, some of these people under deep hypnosis also remember their training in this time between lives where they would practice what to us would seem magical arts of creation. Some of those deeply hypnotized also would recall souls in their cluster group, who had evolved as light beings to higher colors of light and moved beyond their groups, or had become group leaders themselves.

Perhaps, in a sense, we are cocreators of our universe. We most certainly create our own reality to a large extent through our perception of what we consider reality. In that sense, we create our own existence. Of course, this requires a sense of awareness. To become masters of the universe, or masters of time and space, we would require a heightened state of awareness through a heightened sense of consciousness. Perhaps in a Jungian sense we collectively create our universe, our very existence, through our collective unconscious.

Such creative powers, ethically speaking, probably should be governed by the highest intent, concerned with the greatest good for the whole. Certainly highly evolved spiritual beings can see the connectedness and interrelationship of all life and how all parts of life compose the whole of creation. We are a part of this wheel of life, spokes on the hub. We turn as the seasons turn, and as the tides turn in the cycles of life. All of life spins with us. The squirrels in the trees outside our homes spin on the same wheel, as they gather their few necessary provisions for the winter, or rear their families in the spring when the tree branches are flush with new life. The birds outside our windows are spinning on the same wheel with us, as they watch for danger of the next storm challenging their fragile nests. But unlike the timid birds and squirrels that share our world, we are sitting on the hub of the wheel of life, and we can make sweeping changes. What changes we make often affect their fragile existence, as well as our own. It's an awesome responsibility to be on the hub of existence and a tremendous opportunity.

So how would you stretch time? Of course, it would depend on the situation. If you use this ability to seize the moment, you could use it in the case of an emergency or a trying time when you really want time to pass quickly, or else give yourself longer to respond. There are also times of agony and pain that you want to pass mercifully fast by your perception of the situation. On the other hand, there are moments of intense pleasure that you might want to stretch as long as you are able. In moments of opportunity, such as sports challenges, you might want to manipulate time through your perceptive abilities and heightened awareness, to maximize your potential to make a winning performance. On the other hand, you could use your heightened state of consciousness to travel amazing distances, or visit out-of-this-world places. Once you have these abilities, your choices and your opportunities are almost endless.

You are really only limited by your imagination and your ability to reach a heightened state of consciousness. In this state of being, you are free from the physical restraints of your body and the restraints of the physical universe. Time has no real meaning in the nonphysical world. You have literally all of the time in the world at your disposal to use as you see fit. Like all freedoms and all gifts, however, you will want to use this ability wisely. As you travel in this free-form existence, you are both the student and the teacher. You are the enthusiastic child who is coloring outside the lines, so to speak, so better have a sense of your own art and how you want it to turn out.

I was struck only recently how the greatest athletes manipulate time through their perceptive awareness. It was during the Saint Louis Rams football game on October 15, 2000. The television commentator was remarking how Rams star quarterback Kurt Warner seemed to perform better in game situations than during practice, according to his coach, and seemed to see everything in a game situation "in slow motion."

Clearly, this is an advantage for him. It would be an advantage for anyone to stop the world or at least make everything appear to move in slow motion. It would give you time to analyze the situation and the actions of everyone and everything around you. It gives you extra time to determine your actions in a pressure situation. This would work as well in business or driving your car in traffic, as much as in sports.

Star athletes, however, have become our cultural heroes. They do provide great examples of peak performers who excel in pressure situations. But athletes on a playing field cannot save children from a burning building or avoid a car crash with a well-timed twist of the wrist, despite their amazing reflexes. Sports, after all, are just games we play on a certain field.

To be a real hero, you need to be in the right place at the right time and ready to help. You have to be alert and acutely aware of the situation around you. Everyone reading this book has the opportunity to become a real hero, a greater hero than any sports great on a ball field. It means being totally "plugged in" to real-life situations with all of your wits about you. It means living at a high level of conscious awareness.

For the highly conscious and perceptive person, there are also new worlds to explore. Such a person needn't live in a small box or sandbox. A person with perceptive awareness can explore worlds within worlds by entering a state of higher consciousness. Have you ever wondered what Jesus Christ really meant when he said that heaven is within you? He wasn't encouraging people to build a tipsy, tall tower of Babel to reach heaven. Physical structures, after all, have limitations. People who can reach a higher state of consciousness do not. Dante's epic *The Divine Comedy* also suggests levels of heaven and hell that could be explored in a state of higher consciousness. This is a personal journey that does not require tall towers, ladders, or secret tunnels. It is not a physical journey, but a journey of spirit.

Countless people everywhere make this journey into the world of spirit almost daily. Shamans, yogis, Zen Buddhists, and Eckists represent but a few of the many groups of people who experience the non-ordinary worlds of higher consciousness. I'm also reminded of Sybil Leek who, in *Diary of a Witch,* said that future explorers who travel outside the Earth might be surprised to find that a witch had been there first. Of course, she did not mean they'd reach these distant destinations by rocket ship, but by astral travel in a heightened state of consciousness. Now even modern science suggests that there are realities within realities and universes within universes, separated by only the narrowest of folds in space.

There are many very practical applications for the sort of mind-boggling travel that higher consciousness affords. One can access the fabled Akashik Records where all information on all subjects past, present, and future is stored. Psychics and mystics throughout the centuries have explored the Akashik Records. In addition, one can explore the nonphysical world of spirit where angels, devas, saints, and nature spirits live.

Curiously, one of the most practical applications of this sort of astral travel may be healing the physical body. Indeed, there are models for distance healing and also personal aid. We have already seen how people in a heightened state of awareness can heal through the projection of thought forms. Modern physicists are beginning to see thought projections as a form of energy, so even pragmatists with little belief in mysticism or magic must recognize the energized possibilities of thought forms when properly directed. Distance healing is also possible in an out-of-body experience or astral travel that one can establish through heightened perception and a shift to higher consciousness. In that state, a person is not restricted by physical limitations, since this is a nonphysical world.

Dr. Erik Peper, in researching the state of empathic healers who transfer energy to others in therapeutic touch, concluded such healers indeed reach a level of heightened alertness, which he classified as rapid beta brain activity. This is a state of "superalertness" similar to the keen alertness that Zen masters have been observed to reach in closed-eye meditations. In this state, the healer is acutely focused on one thought or activity, tuning out all peripheral distractions.

You can also heal or comfort yourself in this manner. In this heightened state of consciousness, you can focus on any area of pain or injury and send healing energy to that area in thought forms. Similarly, you can use your hands to help or to heal, using your hands to project and conduct that healing energy, as Dr. Dolores Krieger describes in her book *The Therapeutic Touch*. She used her book to train more than a hundred thousand nurses and other healing professionals around the world.

Many people live in chronic, ceaseless pain or discomfort, however. For them, it's a challenge just to manage their pain. Consider, then, how a shift in perceptive awareness can put them into a state of focused consciousness. In that state, it is possible to tune out all distractions and physical sensations. We have seen, after all, how a person deadens physical sensations to focus perceptive awareness and enter a state of heightened consciousness. Simply meditating for them could be an escape from physical pain, for as long as they can sustain this heightened state of consciousness.

This sort of escape from discomfort would also work for people suffering from confinement. Prisoners can enter a heightened state of consciousness through focused perceptive awareness, and escape their surroundings for a time. They can travel in this state, unrestricted by the physical limitations of their surroundings, and enjoy freedom and mobility through astral projection. There is no limit to where they can go in this nonphysical reality, of course, and no time restrictions, either. There is no time in the nonphysical world. A person can experience a whole vacation in a few seconds. As agents of change in control of our nonphysical reality, we control the duration of events we choose to experience.

Certainly, there are practical and noble applications of time manipulation. All are worth practicing, particularly the selfless acts of compassion and healing. Personally speaking, however, I prefer to enter a heightened state of awareness in the "here-and-now" of the immediate world around me. This is the way the ancient shamans often used it. Yes, they would enter the spirit world and bring back helpful information to their people. They would also become one with the world of nature around them. They would speak with the raven and listen to what it said. They would talk to the trees, the wind, and the mountains. Like my friend, the children's author in Oregon, I would like to get to know more trees like Omarr, the inspiration for his many stories. There is more wisdom in the world than the wisdom of people, to be sure, and certainly more to heaven and hell than is written in our philosophies.

Stretching Exercise

You'll need:

- A quiet, secluded room where you can be alone
- Elongated pad for reclining on the floor or a straight-back chair
- Dim lighting
- A watch or clock somewhere in the room, but not near you

Directions

Check and record the time when you begin.

Either lie on your back on a pad on the floor, or sit erect on a straight-back chair, with your feet planted firmly on the ground. (In either event, make certain that your shoes are removed and that you are comfortable with loose-fitting clothes. It would be ideal to find a quiet, secluded room or setting where you are neither uncommonly hot nor cold.)

Let your body become numb, as you enter a state of focused awareness. Be quiet and still. Order your mind to cease all other activities and become still without internal dialogue. Tune out all sounds and distractions around you. As you enter a state of heightened consciousness, focus on one specific area of your body that you would like to feel better. Picture that part of your body only. Send healing thoughts to that part. Energize your thoughts with a projection of your will. Be conscious of the will center in the abdominal area of your body. Picture energy pulsing from your will center toward the area of your body that you are focusing on. Send thoughts of healing green light to surround that area of your body. Energize this green light with your will. Do not stop until you feel this part of your body beginning to tingle, or coming to life from the numbness that has frozen your entire body during this exercise. What does it feel like? Get in touch with that part of your body. Let it talk to you. What does it tell you?

When you have achieved this sensation in that focused part of your body, wait awhile before you get up. Do not get up too suddenly from this heightened state of consciousness. Your body has been fast asleep. Getting up too suddenly can be very unsettling and a little dangerous, somewhat like stumbling half-asleep out of bed.

When you do stand up, check your clock or watch. Note how much time has elapsed since you began. Did it seem that long to you? Did you experience timelessness in this state of heightened consciousness?

CHAPTER 11

Practical applications

Perhaps you'd like some practical applications of heightened awareness and perfect timing. The techniques previously outlined in this book are useful in entering higher states of consciousness to access the nonphysical reality beyond time and space, of course. In this new reality, virtually anything you conceive is possible. You can cope with daily emergency situations and daily challenges where you need extra time and powers that heightened awareness affords you. You can run faster in less time and slow down events when needed by altering your perception of time and space. Some of the greatest athletes apparently do it. Heroic rescue teams do it. You can do it, too.

But what about everyday applications in the mundane, physical world? Here, too, the ability to control our sensory perception, quiet our internal and external chatter, and slow down the world around us through meditation skills and exercise of will can give us practical advantages. You might call these magical coping skills.

You can use these magical coping skills to help you in practical problem-solving, workplace issues, healing, personal growth, and self-discovery. You can use them during those rugged outdoor adventures, recreational challenges, and competitive situations where you must react faster and sharper than the next person in order to excel or simply survive.

The main thing to remember in seeking practical application of time manipulation is that time is really an illusion. It doesn't exist at all, except in our perception of events or things changing. Therefore, you will need to alter your perception. You need to put yourself into an altered state of consciousness. I have recommended throughout this book that you approach a heightened sense of consciousness. To do this, you must "stop" the world by shutting down your sensory intake of sounds, sights, feelings, tastes, and other senses. This eliminates outside distractions for you to focus on the matter at hand. You cannot process all of this information at once and also expect to reach a meditative state that will lead you to alert superconsciousness. You must also still your inner voices. This includes the endless loop of internal discussion and thoughts that flow through all of our brains, as we mull over the concerns of the day, thoughts of the past, and worries about the future. Stop running the grocery list through your head. Stop worrying about your taxes and checking account. Forget about your busy schedule of tasks ahead of you. Give yourself a time out.

A "time out" is exactly what you'll get if you can meditate and reach a state of heightened consciousness. You will find a time out of place, a time out of synch with the rest of the hubbub that we call the real world. You can reach a level of conscious awareness. The only way to experience timelessness as a human being is to shut down the animal sensations and enter a purely conscious realm. There are no clocks in the realm of higher consciousness and no timekeepers. You are beyond time and space.

Many people who have attempted to meditate never reach this timeless reality because of two basic flaws. One mistake they make is that they never truly shut down all sensory distractions, both externally and internally. This requires a discipline, to be sure, but is not that difficult. Failed meditators often try very hard, but a little part of them is still

holding onto thoughts and senses that they decide they can't live without even temporarily. Perhaps they fear that they will lose themselves if
they let go of their senses. This fear results from the body's refusal to
admit that it can't live without the surrounding sounds, sights, and feelings of the immediate environment. You might call this a survival
mechanism of sorts. It's really just the physical self's domination of the
spirit self, as it holds you fast in place. In a sense, then, we become prisoners of ourselves, foolishly filling both roles of captor and captured.
The solution is to simply tell yourself that the physical self will be fine
during your out-of-body departure into consciousness. Once you
assure yourself that your physical body will be safely tucked away during your adventure into the uncharted world of higher consciousness,
then every cell of your body will accept this truth with assurance and
accept the rest with grace. During this altered state, your heart will
automatically pump and your lungs will automatically work, as well.
Ordinarily, there is no alarm over bodily safety.

The other mistake of would-be meditators is the false belief that
serious meditation must take place under ideal settings. They make a
big deal out of the process. They believe that they need a quiet meditation room, insulated from the world. They think they need special
enhancements such as bells, incense, candles, or special wall treat-
ments to help them reach a state of heightened awareness. In reality,
none of this is necessary and only prepares the would-be meditator
for failure in establishing circumstances that preoccupy the mind and
get in the way of meditating.

The real problem is that we think too much. The real solution to
all of this is just to ask the analytical brain to get out of the way for
awhile and take a well-needed rest from the petty worries of the day.
The Buddhists have a wonderful saying that "the mind is the slayer of
the mind." By that they mean that the mind must convince itself to
step aside and open the gate.

There is natural confusion in mediation over of the mind's role
in shutting down and the conscious mind's role in leaving the body.
To resolve this dilemma, think instead of the analytical mind that

calculates your checkbook and remembers appointments as your brain. In a sense, too, it is your petty dictator who seeks to control your life. It is reluctant to acknowledge anything beyond the physical body that is just a part of you. On the other hand, think of your conscious mind or consciousness as your higher self. It can operate independent of your body. It can even leave your body. This is your spirit, your soul, your life essence.

You can meditate anywhere and reach a state of heightened consciousness and timelessness. You could meditate and reach this state of higher awareness and timelessness while washing the dishes or sitting on the divan. Short of meditating in traffic or any other dangerous spots where your physical body could be in peril, you can do this just about anywhere or anytime. And the more you practice the outlined procedure correctly, the easier it will become for you to reach this timeless state in any situation that confronts you.

Surely, star athletes in action do not stop everything that they are doing to sit down in perfect posture and slowly numb their bodies to enter this state. They have learned to do it within the flow of events. They pop in and out of this state, as needed. They do it quickly and almost effortlessly with practice. It becomes a learned behavior. Soon your total self will sense the opportunity or need and shift you to that new, higher level of consciousness. Then everything slows down in front of you, so that you can react.

Remember that you control time as you experience it. As an agent of change, you control the only real measure of time. This is because time only occurs with change. The theatre of events around us is interpreted by our personal perception of change. Your perception will be somewhat different from mine, although we might agree on many things we observe together. Because of your unique perception, you create your own reality. You also create your own sense of time as an agent of change. Time simply measures change, according to noted physicist Julian Barbour. Beyond that simple function, he said, time is nonexistent. There is really only the "now."

The meditator operates in the "now." He enters a state of timelessness outside the physical world, the realm of physical change, and the illusions that we have about change taking place over time. In the nonphysical state, the meditator can perceive sweeping changes taking place in the twinkling of an eye. And what he perceives and believes with the full force of his will, the meditator can achieve to change his reality.

The beauty of this simple truth is that you, as a meditator, would not need to posture yourself in a sitting trance or set up an elaborate meditation exercise to enter heightened awareness and affect sweeping change. You can enter this state at will and make sweeping changes immediately, once you are accustomed to shifts in consciousness.

You can do this in your everyday life in ways that will free you from weighty problems and complex challenges. Let's look at a few examples of practical applications.

Problem-Solving

Creative problem-solving is much easier in a state of higher consciousness. This is because it involves your focused, higher mind—as opposed to your distracted, lower mind or physical brain. Also, the nonphysical world of higher consciousness that you access with your higher mind contains all of the wisdom of the universe that can be tapped. Like radio waves that leave their sources and float endlessly in the air above us, all thoughts and words ever uttered continue to bounce about forever. After all, they are energy waves and boundless. Think of this as the great brain in space or the collective unconscious, as psychologist Carl Jung called it.

This great brain is not hard to access. When you put yourself into a state of higher consciousness, your mind is alert, focused, and searching outside yourself for information. This is somewhat like extending an antenna high into the sky where the greatest number of incoming signals can reach it. You are really "plugged in" when your higher mind enters this state of higher consciousness. (In contrast, you are really "plugged up" in a limiting way, when you are operating normally within your analytical mind or brain.) In attempting to solve complex problems, there is really no comparison between the limited power of your physical brain and the higher mind with its antenna raised into higher consciousness.

Many artists who are looking for ideas often enter a state of meditation and access the vast library of available information. Sometimes this gives them great insight. Sometimes they parrot back previously composed literature or musical scores, not realizing that they have heard compositions from the past. In this realm, beyond the illusions of our physical world, there is no past, of course. Every note, word, or thought ever conceived continues to exist in the eternal "now." (This can confuse musicians, for instance, who believe that they have personally created a new masterpiece, only to find they had lifted it from somewhere beyond their memory.)

Imagine having access to the greatest thinkers of all history to help you solve your problems and clarify your own thoughts. And your access isn't limited to the vast body of thoughts by men and women. All utterances and thoughts as focused energy waves continue to exist in the universal consciousness and can be accessed by you in a state of higher consciousness. This includes the thoughts of other animals. This includes the thoughts of spirits. It could include the faery realm, the angelic realm, and worlds beyond our immediate comprehension. Higher consciousness gives you access to all levels of reality in all worlds. It can even plug you into the divine.

Let's assess what special features higher consciousness gives you to aid in creative problem-solving.

Special Features

- Clear, focused mind in higher consciousness
- Higher mind operating, as opposed to lower mind or brain
- Access in higher consciousness to previous human thoughts and words
- Access to the thoughts of all other animals

- Access to the thoughts of other realms and realities beyond our physical world

Some people enter higher consciousness to access the fabled Akashik Records, where mystics throughout the ages have believed all records are stored. All knowledge is kept there. Of course, this is not a physical structure. You can only enter it by traveling beyond your body in pure consciousness.

All of the limitless body of knowledge and ideas you can access in the state of heightened awareness can be used in creative problem-solving. Your most complex puzzles can be solved or at least addressed by overlaying the questions you have over this vast matrix of answers.

Let's assume, for instance, that you are trying to solve a complex structural design question. Maybe you want to build new steps for your house; or maybe you want to design a bridge in a manner that is completely alien to you. Simply get into the meditation mode and raise your antenna into heightened consciousness. Once you reach heightened attention, you can tap into heightened awareness. This higher antenna gives you clear reception of all channels and all signals ever released into the collective unconscious.

You can tap into Archimedes and Frank Lloyd Wright, for starters. Or maybe your problem is mathematical. Try tapping into the eternal thoughts and words of Einstein. If your questions are more basic, try accessing Plato.

Inventors are a resourceful lot. They take a very creative approach to solving complex problems. The ones I have interviewed as a news-paper and magazine reporter had one thing in common, however. They all dismissed the everyday way in which people routinely view the world. The real problem, they told me, was the way we perceive things. So they attempt to get beyond normal perception. They also meditate on the problem and spend quiet, thoughtful hours alone focused on the problem.

That's where creative solutions come. Creative-problem solving is best done in quiet with the opportunity to focus only on that problem from various, intentional approaches. It's done in meditation, focusing the problem in your mind. Deeper meditation takes you into heightened awareness where you can access limitless information to bear on the problem.

The trick to tapping into the universal consciousness for problem-solving is simply to focus on the question. Clear your mind of everything else. Allow your higher mind to focus only on the question at hand, as your consciousness begins to leave your body and drift into the vast unknown of eternal wisdom. The mind must be clear, so do not work the problem in your mind or attempt to dissect it. Simply hold the question in your mind as a mental image as you enter into higher consciousness. Put your will or focus behind the question to drive it. Remember, you cannot analyze or work problems in your head as you enter this subconscious state. Your mind must be clear. You are simply bringing a picture along with you on your way into the higher consciousness realms. You are leaving your body with an agenda. Perhaps you would prefer to consider this a posthypnotic suggestion to yourself to bring this agenda with you. Whatever you do, you must remember not to mull the question over in your head, or you will not be able to clear your lower mind to meditate and enter higher consciousness. You are transferring an image from the lower mind to the higher mind. The higher mind can take your image on a journey of discovery, only if you put your will behind it and drive it with focused intent.

I have used this techniques many times in solving complex problems. I have used it on financial questions, personal difficulties, home repair matters, and even creative shortcomings of an artistic nature. Once I used it to write a poem. The words came to me effortlessly from a voice that whispered to me in the quiet. eternal void beyond the chair where I sat meditating. When I returned to my body, the words were still with me. They were a little like Robert Browning, but also the way a faun might view things. Perhaps there was a little bit of a muse involved in the words. The poem was quickly published and republished. But, really, I was more the scribe than the poet. Or maybe I was a collaborator. The voices in the collective unconscious are willing to collaborate and share thoughts and ideas. They will even give you words, if you ask.

Try this simple exercise for problem-solving in a meditative state.

Problem-Solving Exercise

You'll need:
- A quiet room
- A straight-back chair or solid pad on which to recline, face up
- No other people or animals in the room

Directions

1. Sit upright in the chair with shoes off and feet solidly on the floor. If you use a reclining pad instead of a chair, lie on your back, with shoes off and hands to your side in an attentive, yet relaxed posture.

2. Put yourself in a meditative state by relaxing the body and letting it become numb.

3. Shut down your senses.

4. Tune out all external and internal distractions.

5. Think of a problem that has stumped you. Do not analyze it, just recognize it and hold it in your mind like a picture. Do not obsess over it. Your approach here will be to seek outside answers by posing the questions in the realm of higher consciousness.

6. Now clear all thoughts and internal dialogue from your mind, holding only the question in focus as you begin to enter a new state of heightened consciousness and leave your body behind.

7. Now drift into a state of higher consciousness.

(Note: If you do this exercise correctly, you have a good chance of obtaining outside answers to your question. If you are unsuccessful, try again. It's not easy to carry a question with you, as you attempt to clear your mind to enter this higher state of consciousness. You must carry it not foremost in your mind, but only in the back of your mind. The main problem involved here is the very human desire to begin analyzing your question and rehashing old efforts to solve your question. If this happens, your analytical brain is engaged with internal dialogue, and you will be unable to clear your lower mind to engage your higher mind.)

In the Workplace

You also could use higher consciousness to help you in the workplace. While this sounds like a very practical and profitable use of higher consciousness, consider first the setting. Some people work at home without distractions and can quietly meditate by sitting quietly in their living room or home workspace. Most people, however, work in social settings, interacting with coworkers who are always interrupting them during the day as part of the normal routine. People who work in a cubicle or open setting with many coworkers nearby at all times might find it particularly difficult to meditate.

Let's consider two common situations in the workplace and resolve how to meditate in both of them. The first situation is the crowded, noisy office or factory setting where meditation might seem difficult. The second situation would be those opportune times when you are away from your coworkers for a brief time.

Crowded work settings or places where you are easily interrupted pose problems for anyone who would attempt to slip into a state of higher consciousness to access information. Nonetheless, these problems can be overcome. One technique that I have personally found effective in these situations is to take a little rest break or a coffee break with as much privacy as possible and tell people that I need to "rest my eyes" for a few minutes. Or I might say that I have a little yoga exercise or self-hypnosis exercise that relaxes me and quickly rejuvenates me during a hectic day. That's all very true, of course.

With this approach, it's also good to put a sign that says something like "Do not disturb" on your door, if you have a private office.

Of course, many people cannot take a rest break during the course of their work day and even find coffee breaks and lunch breaks to be less than private with interruptions or lack of privacy. Even in these situations, however, a person should be able to enter a state of heightened awareness momentarily. The trick is simply to become so practiced in the techniques of meditation that you can clear your head of internal and external distractions, tune our your senses, and enter a state of heightened consciousness at a moment's notice. Some athletes do it all the time within the hectic pace of a game. The practiced meditator can quickly tune in and tune out whenever desired. You can do it standing up, sitting down, or even walking if necessary.

The lucky people are the people who work independent of coworkers, if only temporarily. They can easily find quiet places all alone to meditate during the business day. This would include people who work at home, people who work alone, and people who travel away from their office or factory coworkers even part of the time.

All people can access higher consciousness with work-related questions in the same way they can meditate and activate the higher mind for answers to personal problems. Nobody working alone has all of the answers. The human brain is limited to our training, native intelligence, and ability to size up situations as they present themselves. Even companies pulling together in the best spirit of teamwork will have puzzling problems that cripple their success during the business day. Human brain power is limited. On the other hand, the collective unconscious, which any person can tap in a state of heightened awareness during meditation, is limitless in terms of information. The only real question is whether you can reach a pure state of heightened consciousness to reach it.

So how would you apply this technique to creative problem-solving in the workplace? Well, let's say that you are an architect who wants to design something that nobody (to your knowledge) has ever attempted. There is no blueprint. You need to create it. Where do you turn? Or perhaps you need to come up with a number quickly, but lack some of the information that you need to devise a formula to help you determine the number. Sometimes in the workplace today we need to think on our feet with limited information, or we are doomed.

Insight is what is needed. Did you ever consider where the quick-thinkers get their sudden insight? Insight suggests that you look inside yourself for answers. It suggests a different kind of sight, other than the physical information around you. This means shutting down your senses, shutting down external and internal distractions, and getting quiet inside yourself. It means quiet reflection. The meditator takes this a step further in turning off the lower mind and activating the higher mind.

Ever hear the term *inspired idea?* Ever wonder where inspired thought comes from? Sometimes it comes from a friend or mentor who inspires you. But what about those flashes of sudden insight that hit a person like a thunderbolt out of nowhere? Such insight probably comes from a lot of quiet time alone, meditating on a problem. If people meditate deeply enough and engage the higher mind, their sudden inspiration probably comes from higher consciousness and the collective bank of knowledge that is available there.

Workplace Sites and Opportunities

Here is a list of optional sites and conditions for entering higher consciousness for problem-solving in the workplace.

- Working alone at home or in private office apart from coworkers
- During travel
- During breaks or lunchtime
- With "Do not disturb" sign on your door or cubicle
- When "resting your eyes" quietly at your desk
- On the fly, with sudden shifts in consciousness during the day

Everyone can engage their higher minds in the workplace with a little practice and focused intent, regardless of the hectic pace and lack of rest periods available at the job site. It just takes practice and will. Simply employ the techniques previously outlined in this book to enter a meditative state and reach higher consciousness. Remember, even a brief second in this altered state can seem like hours, since you are controlling time. You are creating perfect timing or perfecting time manipulation. Time is but an illusion. There is all of the time in the world, if you can focus your intent and control your perception. Make your own reality.

An exercise for various opportunities in the workplace might prove helpful to you:

Exercise for Brief Rest Spots

You'll need:

- A work break or chance to quietly "rest your eyes" awhile
- A chair, if available; otherwise, improvise to find a good seat
- Find setting as quiet as possible and with as few distractions as possible, under the circumstances
- If possible, put a "Do not disturb" sign on your door, if you have one

Directions

1. Put your hands on the arms of the chair and your feet firmly on the ground (best with shoes off). Keep an erect posture.

2. Close your eyes to shut out distractions, or keep them mostly closed.

3. Direct your body to grow numb and dull your senses.

4. Focus on a work problem, without analyzing it. Hold it in your head softly like a beautiful picture to take with you on a journey of discovery.

5. Shut off any internal dialogue or thought.

6. Disregard all outside distractions and clear your head until you hear only silence.

7. Picture the beautiful blackness inside your conscious mind.

8. Leaving your body behind, walk into the void of consciousness.

9. Wait patiently to listen and see what higher consciousness brings to you.

(Note: You will find this a relaxing break in your hectic work day and probably helpful in solving nagging work problems, as well. Don't think of it as wasting time during the work day. With practice, this little exercise takes very little time, as others perceive it. Think of this exercise as a creative way to think through your problems by engaging your higher mind to meditate on work issues.)

Self-Discovery and Growth

The journey beyond the body is a journey of discovery. It is beyond your lower mind or the brain you use for simple analysis in the physical world. This journey also can be used for more basic exploration of personal growth and self-discovery.

Wouldn't you like to discover who you really are and what your purpose in life really is all about? Wouldn't you like to explore possible past lives? Perhaps you'd like to gain a broader perspective about yourself and how you can grow as a person.

Your higher mind can take you on a journey of self-discovery and personal growth that can give you real answers to these questions that are beyond your ability to analyze. Remember, there is an infinite amount of information available in higher consciousness. This information can be used in many practical ways, including personal growth and self-discovery.

I have personal experience in using higher consciousness in this practical manner. One time, I explored my past lives. Another time, I sought clarification of my purpose in life or life mission. Yet another time, I sought assistance to become a more engaging person. In all efforts, I was successful in receiving helpful, practical information of a personal nature from the universal consciousness. I found that if you focus on a question and bring it with you into higher consciousness, you will receive answers that are simply beyond us as physical beings.

My probes into possible past lives brought vivid scenes of former lives I had lived. In posing the question about past lives, I had no idea what sort of answers I would receive or how I would receive them. I must admit, however, that I was rather surprises to be dropped into dramatic, telling scenes from my former lives. There's something about putting on your old clothes and meeting old friends and family in familiar surroundings that really brings everything back to you. I have relived scenes in this fashion from an early life as a farmer in Wales, a boy on the losing side of the Trojan War, and a petty criminal in a very early time that I would describe as Lemurian. As I lived key scenes from these past lives again in a state of heightened awareness, I can only say that the experiences were very vivid in exquisite detail. Also, my roles in these scenes from times past were so real and so personal that I have no doubt that I lived these lives.

This approach is remarkably different from deep hypnotic therapy, past-life regression therapy, or even group meditation in which a person in heightened consciousness is directed by someone else in this journey of self-discovery. In personal meditation, a person simply carries this question about past lives into heightened consciousness, without anyone framing or guiding an answer of any sort. The question goes out to the infinite wisdom of the universal consciousness. What answers you receive either ring true, or they do not. If they ring true, every fiber of your being will tingle with the profound realization. Deep down inside you, you already know much of the truth. You only need to have it verified and explained to you. Once you are able to recall it and realize it, you will have no trouble embracing it as true.

If you are able to relive scenes from your past lives, pay close attention to everything you see. Look at the faces. Observe the lay of the land. Read the sign posts. If people speak to you, listen closely to everything they say. Display a dispassionate objectivity in witnessing everything you can, as much as you can. After all, this is your life.

I have learned through experience in meditation that discovering your life purpose or mission works much the same way. I carried questions about my life purpose into heightened consciousness and found myself climbing a mountain without trails every time I did this. Finally, I found my way to the top of the mountain, after several sessions. When I did, I got my answers. I found myself wandering into a cave where two old monks in brown robes initiated me and gave me work orders for this life. I was not alone in that cave, either. I witnessed another person receive somewhat similar work orders in the same initiation ceremony. Later, I actually met this other person in the physical universe and was able to verify the reality of the experience. She looked like the woman in my past-life memory, but I did not reveal this to her. Then one day, she told me that she was haunted by vivid dreams of "priests in brown robes" in an experience so powerful and meaningful to her that she had always wanted to paint the scene. It was pretty much the same memory that I had.

The other practical way I have employed heightened consciousness was to improve myself as a person. The question I carried with me loosely into heightened awareness was how to become more engaging as a person. Actually, I have done this many times. Every time I pose this question, I seem to get different help on aspects of self-improvement. Each experience has one thing in common, however. They are all dramatic scenes in which the answer is acted out for me. This provides a dramatic demonstration of how the "new, improved me" should interact. Role-playing really is a great way to learn something new. The last time I did this sort of role-playing for self-improvement, I learned how to be witty and charming in a way that people like and trust. I found that to be very different from act-ing funny in a broad sense. Other times, I have found myself in the middle of a passion play. These scenes are all very telling, once you live them.

There is a built-in safety mechanism to ensure that this approach is both valid and meaningful. Without it, a person could doubt that an experience in higher consciousness was pertinent to personal self-development or self-discovery. That safety mechanism is your focused intent. You enter a state of heightened awareness with the intent to learn something about yourself. Your higher mind brings this question with you into universal consciousness and poses this question to the infinite wisdom of the universe. In a real sense, then, you have programmed your own journey into self-discovery and should meet with success at some point in your efforts.

Never doubt what spirit teaches you in these journeys. Never doubt yourself and what you have seen during heightened awareness. It is meaningful and significant for you. Spirit does not toy with you, nor should you toy with spirit. Such trivial mind games are not played in heightened awareness. If the meaning or significance of something you have seen in heightened consciousness is not readily apparent to you, do not attempt to analyze it during normal consciousness in your body. Your lower mind or brain cannot process this information and may only trivialize it. You must meditate on the meaning of your journeys into self-discovery until the truth is obvious to you and the truth resonates within every fiber of your being.

Self-discovery is the most important thing most of us will ever undertake. And it's a lot more complicated than looking into a mirror or getting constructive feedback from respected friends. It's learning who you really are, deep down. It's learning how we got here and where we are going. More importantly, it's learning why we are here.

Now, you can tone your body, dress well, and master interpersonal skills to get along well in life. None of that, however, answers the nagging, fundamental questions that everyone seeks to answer at some point: Who am I, really? Why am I here? Only a journey of self-discovery can begin to find the answers to these questions. In classical literature, the hero undertakes a challenging journey that forces him (or her) into self-discovery along the way. The hero's journey is what all of us need to take in order to find ourselves and our life purpose. That journey can be taken through higher consciousness without ever leaving your home.

Here's an exercise you might find helpful for meditating on self-discovery.

Self-Discovery Exercise

You'll need:
- Quiet room where you can sit alone
- A straight-back chair on which to sit

Directions

1. Remove your shoes to plant your feet firmly on the ground.

2. Close your eyes.

3. Detach yourself from all sounds internal and external to you.

4. Detach yourself from sensory awareness.

5. Breathe deeply and slowly through one nostril, and then the other.

6. Allow your body to grow numb.

7. Hold a picture of what you want to know. You might ask who you really are. Or you might ask what is your life purpose.

8. Shut down all thinking, taking only this question with you.

9. When you feel totally calm, quiet, and at peace, then you will enter higher consciousness with great ease. Do not force it. Wait for it to happen.

(Note: Did you receive any sort of answer to your basic question? If not, keep trying. Part of the trick here is not to try too hard. It's an exercise in detachment to want something for all the right reasons and not want it with great passion. It is amazingly easy to become obsessed and attached with your past lives without putting them into proper perspective, for instance.)

Health and Healing

You also can use heightened consciousness to improve your health and well-being. I can personally attest to this. One of the first workshops that I ever attended on consciousness and meditation was held at Camp Indralaya on Orcas Island, Washington, in the mid-1980s. The instructor was a Seattle musician who maintained that notes and colors as vibrations or energy waves could affect our health in positive ways. He also believed that certain sounds and colors activated certain chakras in the body to activate the positive flow of energy in the body.

The most fascinating part of the workshop for me, however, was a meditation exercise he led. Ordinarily, I don't like group meditations for the simple reason that they are directed and therefore manipulated by the person who is leading the meditation. In that sense, they are limiting as to what a person might experience without the power of suggestion from the group leader who acts very much like a hypnotist in leading subjects through a hypnotic session. In all honestly, however, a skillful meditation leader can guide a roomful of people into higher consciousness where they are all released to have totally separate, individualized experiences.

This group leader at the Theosophical island camp was such a remarkable meditation leader. He asked us to lie down on our backs on mats with our shoes off. There were a lot of us in the room, so we were positioned head to toe in close proximity. I remember having somebody's socks on one side of my head and another person's head on the other side of me.

Our leader told us to close our eyes, if we felt more comfortable that way and believed it would help us meditate. He told us to clear our mind and be still, observing nothing but the sound of his voice.

Then he told all of us to picture ourselves in some setting where we felt very comfortable and strong. He allowed time for us to focus on that. Then he told us to surround ourselves in this ideal setting with a color that we considered a healing color. He allowed time for us to visualize this. Then he told us to select a part of our body where we wanted to focus our healing attention. Of course, this was different for each one of us. He left the details to each of us to determine.

In my case, I put myself on a cliff that overlooked an ocean. The cliff was a green hillside for the most part, with a few trees and boulders. I selected green as a good healing color and surrounded myself in this setting with green.

When I selected the part of my body that I wanted to heal, I chose my left ankle. I had twisted it a little from running to attend the group meditation session. So I focused on "left ankle." It was a little hard for me to locate my left ankle in the crowd, with so many ankles and arms everywhere around me. It didn't help that I felt so separated from my physical body in this state of higher consciousness.

After a good, long time for everyone to focus healing attention on appropriate parts of their bodies, the group leader asked us to slowly return to normal consciousness. It took some of us a long time to get back into our bodies without feeling disoriented. I remember trying to stand up and clumsily falling down again. My feet had fallen asleep; and the rest of me was pretty unstable, too.

Our leader asked us whether we felt differently or noticed any signs of success in our healing efforts on our bodies. It was a sort of rhetorically question that he did not expect to have anyone answer aloud. In different parts of the room, however, many individuals started chatting with people near them about their personal experiences. Soon the room was abuzz with small group chatter.

I remarked to people near me that I had tried to affect my left ankle. At times, I felt it tingle a little. I wasn't sure that I had focused on my left ankle the whole time, however. When I said this, I noticed a young woman in the crowd who was straining to hear me better.

"Your left ankle?" she asked. "That's strange! I couldn't think of anything to do. Then all of a sudden, my left ankle started to tingle and feel warm."

I asked where her feet were positioned during the floor exercise. Her ankle had been very close to the position of my ankle in the tangle of arms and legs. After we discussed this awhile, there was little doubt in either of our minds that I had affected the tingling, warm sensation in her ankle in my feeble attempt to direct healing energy down to my own ankle near hers. It did demonstrate to us, however, just how powerful this sort of healing can be in sending energy.

This sort of healing exercise in a state of heightened consciousness works for a number of reasons. The most obvious to those of us at the healing workshop was the use of thought forms directed at an ailing part of the body. Thought forms are generated by the higher mind and sent to a target. Accuracy, as we learned in our exercise, is something that comes with practice. Our thought forms are actually energy waves.

If you think that accuracy should be easy in sending such energy waves, compare them to waves in the ocean. Waves in the ocean are also energy waves, but can take many shapes, directions, and velocities. Some waves can disperse broadly or have a tight pattern. Others can thunder like breaking surf, or roll gently under or over the surface of the water. The champions at sending energy waves under water are probably the orca whales who can send a narrow beam to strike a target hard at great distances. That's pinpoint accuracy in sending personal energy waves.

Thought forms, of course, can be used for many purposes. Our purpose is not to blast salmon out of the water for dinner. Our purpose here is to direct thought forms for healing. It takes practice to get this right. Once you get the right feel for it, you will send healing thought forms at will. How do you do this? Send your thought form with love. Also, remember how you feel whenever you feel well and safe. There is a wave frequency for healing, just as there is a frequency for destruction, according to renowned researcher Dr. Andrija Puharich. Send your thought form for healing with a frequency that you associate with love and compassion, and you can't go wrong. A mother knows this instinctively, when she kisses a toddler's skinned elbow to make it feel better. Deep down inside you, you know this healing frequency, too.

Another thing that makes healing possible in a state of heightened consciousness is the use of intent. If you focus on your intent to heal, you can accurately hit the target every time. In a real sense, intent is a magical principle. It is also familiar to anyone who can recognize the force of the human will. What makes some people inwardly strong is their will. They have great will power. They have a strong will to live. They drive home their points with a strong presence, marked by their will to succeed. It is our human force, a very basic power that is recognized by the most successful among us.

When a person focuses on a target with intention, thought forms become thought power. They become more energized by our driving power of will behind them. Thought power can affect changes. It can bend metal. It can mend bones. It can transform things. But it must be directed with the right intent. I can send thought power to you to help you heal. You can send thought power to me to help me heal. We also can work cooperatively to help our planet heal.

I often think about a friend of mine in Sioux Falls who claims to be the seventh daughter of a Lakota medicine woman. She told me once that she got together regularly with other medicine women to help heal a crack in an atomic power plant that they feared would go unnoticed and unattended by plant personnel. In meditations together, they sensed the malady and then worked together to send their healing thoughts to repair it. To my knowledge, they have suffered no power plant disaster to this day. Many witches worked together in this fashion during the Second World War, it has been noted, to help bring down the Nazi reign of power.

Thought power can affect change. Collectively, it can overcome armies. There is another aspect of healing in higher conscious that is just as important as thought forms or focused intent. This is the principle of subtle bodies. We must remember that we are more than our physical bodies, even though that is the first place we look when we find symptoms of ailing health. The physical body is our dense body. The health aura or etheric body surrounds this physical body like an envelope. Beyond that, we have a mental body and a causal body, as well. If the outer bodies with their own chakra energy vortexes were to develop imbalances or energy flow problems, those problems manifest eventually in the physical body. Everything eventually falls to earth. Everything that comes to us begins outside of us, but eventually impacts our bodies. That is true, also, of illness and disease.

The energy work I have done in training with Dr. Dolores Krieger and Dora Kunz has really convinced me that the subtle bodies that surround our physical bodies have a lot to do with our health. They need attention, too. Energy healing addresses the subtle bodies in ways that conventional medicine can't do. Naturally, energy healing cannot replace conventional medicine that addresses the physical condition. Nonetheless, it assists in unseen ways in helping people to heal themselves. Sometimes it helps by creating a soothing sense of well-being and comfort level whereby real healing can take place.

The healing recommended in this book is not meant to replace the important care of a qualified physician, but rather to supplement it by creating a favorable condition for healing. Think of this as a "toning" of the body or putting the body in proper tone. Moreover, the healing recommendation in this book is intended for the reader to use personally, rather than on another person. Also, you can use thought forms, focused intention, and energy healing on your pets and houseplants. Send them your good thoughts. Thoughts can help a body heal.

My favorite personal use of healing in heightened consciousness is to avoid pain. Let me explain that I don't like pain. When I sit in the dentist's chair, I avoid the pain of needles and drilling. I put myself into a state of heightened consciousness and leave my body behind. I put myself on a sandy beach with a tropical drink in one hand and suntan lotion in the other. When the doctor tells me the drilling is all over, I fold up my chaise lounge and slowly return to my body (I don't return too quickly, because I don't want to feel my mouth all at once). Yes, I have been known to smile when I climb out of the dentist's chair. After all, the beach on the Caribbean is always sunny, and the sky as blue as the water. If you could go anywhere you want instead of the dentist's office, why not pick the Caribbean?

Perhaps an exercise like my Orcas Island healing workshop would prove helpful to you:

Healing Meditation Exercise

You'll need:

- Quiet, isolated room (if available); otherwise, improvise
- A mat, or reasonably comfortable yet firm floor surface
- To dim the lights, but it is not essential

Directions

1. Remove your shoes and get comfortable. Loose fitting clothes are best.

2. Lie on your back with your arms comfortable at your sides or folded in front of you. Your legs are straight. Lie quietly and without motion.

3. Become very quiet. Tune out the internal dialogue and thoughts inside your head and tune out all exterior sounds and distractions. Let your physical body grow numb. Tune out all sensory perception. Breathe slowly and deeply.

4. Clear all thoughts and feeling and wait for a shift to higher consciousness. Wait until you see blankness inside your head as a starting point for your consciousness experience.

5. You are going to a place of great power and comfort for yourself, where all things are possible beyond time and space. You will be wrapped in healing colors to assist you in the task ahead.

6. You are seen by helpful spirits beyond the physical plane. They will assist you on your noble mission.

7. Carry with you only one thought. Carry an image of the part of you that you would like to affect with healing energy. Perhaps you have a sore foot or a strained muscle. Or perhaps you would like to send healing energy to a sick pet or a favorite houseplant or tree that needs help in healing itself. If so, carry an image of that pet, plant, or sore foot improving with your focused attention. Do not analyze this situation or process. Only hold it softly as a picture you intend to carry with you on a journey.

8. Now enter higher consciousness, softly carrying this image with you. You will reappear in a world beyond time and space, where all things are possible.

(Note: Did you see your power spot when you entered higher consciousness? And did you see colored light wrapped around you? Perhaps you heard healing music, as well. If so, did you also see the ailing subject that you intended to assist with your healing thought form? How did that go? Did your subject appear to respond to your assistance? If none of this appeared to you in your out-of-body experience in higher consciousness, it could be that you sent your thought form without leaving your body to visit your ailing subject. If you were attempting to send healing energy to one of your own legs or arms, of course, you didn't really need to step very far outside your body. If none of this seemed to happen for you, practice this exercise and variations that seem right to you until you do get results that are vivid experiences for you. All of this is within your power. You are an agent for change and a master of time and space in higher consciousness.)

Competitive and Recreational Sports

We already have seen how many sports stars appear able to control time in critical situations to achieve performance excellence. Swimmers and sprinters go as fast as they can throughout a race, but in the final seconds often seem to go twice as fast in a final burst of speed. Batters appear able to slow down 100-mile-per-hour fastballs and see the ball larger than life. Basketball scoring aces stop down action in the blurring confusion around them to make their moves, as though everything is moving around them in slow motion. The premise here is that superstars know how to enter states of heightened awareness by stopping the world around them and entering the timeless state of higher consciousness. This is perfect timing.

The nonprofessional athlete and recreational athlete also can profit from the practical application of perfect timing. You don't have to be a professional athlete or superstar to practice meditation and enter the timeless state of heightened consciousness. You do, however, need to practice these shifts in consciousness so that you can make the transition at a moment's notice. The blurring distractions of an athletic event make it difficult to quiet the mind and stop the world around you to enter a meditative state. This is especially true in competitive situations. If you can't manipulate the moment by selectively stopping down things around you and quickly shifting between states of consciousness, you could find yourself slammed against the wall in a hockey game. It requires precise, disciplined control. You must be an impeccable warrior or warrior athlete to pull this off. Practice plenty before you try this in the heat of a game.

Learning to pop into heightened consciousness and pop out again in a hectic situation like a game requires staged implementation. You can't suddenly switch off your physical body and switch on higher consciousness and expect to function in the flow of a game. If you watch top athletes who gets into this "zone," as sports people often call it, you will notice that their eyes seem to glaze over or close halfway for a brief time. They might even appear to be going into a trance. That trance, of course, is the altered state of consciousness known to meditators. They sort of "tune out" all the peripheral distractions that don't matter to them. They do this very selectively. Then they go into a state of higher consciousness very briefly. Of course, a split second can seem to last much longer to a person in this state, because there is no time or normal laws of physics in higher consciousness. This is a supreme effort in selective perception.

The trick, of course, is for athletes to make snap decisions on the run as to what perception to maintain. Certainly, they would need to maintain sight and feel in order to function in an athlete event. Perhaps they focus on running and tune out most everything else around them. So they keep a part of the physical body operating with new orders being generated by the higher mind. Well, that's really only half of the trick. The other part to the trick is to turn the higher mind on and then turn it off, while staying physically in control within the flow of the game.

Most people think that spectacular athletes simply try harder when they "turn it on." Certainly, they do find extra energy and move with greater speed in less time at these moments, almost as though time for them was standing still. These golden moments in an athlete's life are truly magical. They can see everything happening in slow motion around them. They have all the time in the world to make amazing moves. They can run faster, think faster, and jump higher than anyone else. And all of this comes by slipping momentarily into higher consciousness, a nonphysical reality where time does not exist and the normal laws of physics do not apply. What's even better, they operate in these golden moments with a higher mind that thinks faster and better than the analytical mind or brain that people use in normal, physical consciousness.

Many accounts of top athletes who make the most of the moment are described in John Jerome's amazing book, *The Sweet Spot in Time*. Jerome describes his book, moreover, as a classic guide to exploring and reaching your full athletic potential. For anyone who wants to excel in competitive sports, living fully in the moment at critical junctions is the way to expand your possibilities and attain performance excellence.

For the rest of us, it's a way to get the most out of our moments in recreational pursuits. That could be jogging, swimming, tennis, or hiking. Any activity where you perform can be expanded and enriched by a heightened state of awareness that allows you to expand your perception of time and operate somewhat outside of normal physical limitations.

Let me give you an example from one of my favorite recreational activities—hiking. My son and I used to hike on Mt. Hood in Oregon when I managed a newspaper there. Like a lot of hikers, we would sometimes lose track of the hour when we would climb up the mountain in the summer afternoon. Darkness comes early in the woods, since there are no streetlights. Consequently, it's easy to run out of daylight in the middle of a hike in the woods.

That's what happened to us one summer on Mt. Hood. We got as high on the mountain as we could before noticing the sun was already starting to set. We were just having too much fun to notice we were running out of time. It had taken us most of the afternoon to get that high on the mountain; and experience told us that it normally took us about two hours to walk down from that elevation. Consequently, we had a problem. Without flashlights, how could we get back down the mountain in the precious, little time left? We might hurry back, but that could be dangerous on a mountain side with limited light. It would be so easy to slip and fall.

So we took time out to sit and meditate on this little situation. We got very still and tuned out all distractions. We looked inside ourselves for strength and answers. We slowly got up and quietly walked down the mountain without discussion or concern. Surprisingly, we reached the bottom of the mountain in record time and beat the setting sun. My only explanation is that our meditation put us into a state of higher consciousness where all things are possible and time stands still. How else could you explain it?

Another time I was engaged in a little road rally with my sports car. Halfway through the race, I discovered that I was lost. I had overanalyzed the directions and made a mess of navigation. That little brain we use for analytical thought gets us into more trouble at times, doesn't it? Anyway, I drove around aimlessly for hours and later found that even the guys who stood at various checkpoints had called it a day and gone to the finish line for the party and awards ceremony. So I was really lost without even checkpoints. I drove around until I realized I was in the middle of nowhere with dwindling gasoline reserves. I was going to run out of gas in the middle of the woods at night. This is not a pleasant thought, so I considered what to do about it.

I pulled over to the side of the road and cut the engine. That's where I sat in quiet meditation. What do you do when the situation seems physically impossible? I went deep inside myself for answers. This was not the time to panic. So I quieted my mind and tuned out the world for a moment of serious meditation. Once I switched on my higher mind, I knew exactly what to do. I turned on the engine and turned my car around. I drove slowly and deliberately, taking turns without questioning the selection. My higher mind was in control; I drove in a trancelike state. I can't say exactly how long I drove in this state, because time seemed to stand still. At last, I arrived on a stretch of highway with an all-night gas station nearby. I was saved.

Sometimes you need to seize the moment. You do this by getting out of your own way. There is a special part of each one of us that can be tapped at critical moments for superpowers, if you go deep enough inside yourself to find it.

Emergency Situations

The confidence I gained in handling that little road rally experience helped me plenty when I later found myself in a real life-threatening situation on the open road. I was attempting to drive across Montana in the wee hours of the morning during a blizzard. It was below freezing and snowing hard. The roads were extremely icy.

My real problem is that I was running out of gas at 3 A.M. with no service stations in sight. Of course, I could park somewhere and wait for one to open in a few hours. I didn't have enough gas to idle for hours; and I would surely freeze to death without running the car for heat. The situation looked pretty grim.

Then I remembered my road rally experience. So I pulled the car off to the side of the highway and started to meditate. I was really scared this time, but managed to quiet myself and tune out all distractions. When I made the connection to higher consciousness, my higher mind seemed to pluck the answer out of thin air.

I stayed in a state of heightened awareness the rest of the morning drive. I was focused on two points. The first point was basic. I stayed in a state of heightened awareness in order to make my perception of time stand still. How else could I drive for hours in a blizzard with almost no gas left in the tank? I also focused on a magical principle I had observed my Oregon friend Karen do in front of a mirror once. She stood in front of the mirror and made her hair longer and then shorter as we watched, in order to decide how she looked best. The magical feat didn't seem at all outlandish or difficult for her; and she made little of it. I was tremendously impressed, however. I was also inspired. So my second intention that snowy morning in Montana was to stretch the fuel in my gas tank. I got inside the tank with my consciousness and asked the gas to stretch itself, so it wouldn't run out.

If this sounds outlandish to you, how else could you explain how I drove across Montana in a blizzard in the wee hours of the morning with my gas gauge on empty all the way? I had driven all the way from Wyoming on the other side of Yellowstone Park on that tank of gas. I hadn't reasoned that there would be no gas stations open when I reached the middle of Montana in the early morning. In fact, there was nothing open. My gas gauge slowly worked its way down to the empty mark after driving from one state to another. And then the gauge didn't move below empty for several hours. That was a magical time. It was a matter of personal time perception and a focused intent to stay in the "now."

Lost and Found

You also can enter heightened consciousness when you are lost. In such case, you simply give yourself a picture of yourself being lost to carry with you into higher consciousness. The answers will come to you. The higher mind can always find the answer, when the lower mind is befuddled. It simply has more information on which to draw—an infinite universe of information, and all of the time in the world at its disposal. The higher mind works on the problem in a pristine environment, too, unencumbered by the distractions of the mundane world around us and a dependent body that is preoccupied with sensory overload.

You also can find lost objects or lost people by using your higher mind in a meditative state. In such case, you need to picture the person or object you seek and carry that picture softly with you into higher consciousness. Do not analyze the problem, but simply carry the image of the lost item gently and quietly with you into higher consciousness. The answers will come. Usually, you will see the location you seek and then pop back instantly to normal consciousness. The higher mind willingly surrenders control to the physical body when appropriate. It is not jealous of the lower mind in the same way the lower mind often resents the higher mind. The higher mind is more aware of the true nature of things.

Frankly, this is how I find my lost keys, checkbook, and reading glasses these days. I used to go into a panic and tear the house up in a mad search. Sometimes I would badger people with questions about the lost keys or glasses. In this state of panic, I rarely found anything in a hurry. That can cause real problems, of course, especially when you need your keys to drive to work. My approach now is simply to enter a state of higher consciousness and carry a picture of the lost object with me as I enter this altered state for answers. The answers always come. It's truly amazing.

Sometimes it is hard even for the higher mind to readily locate the lost object. In such cases, the higher mind will likely take control of your body and walk you through the steps that are necessary to find the lost object or person. Psychics who find lost people often walk around in a trance-like state when searching in difficult cases. This trance-like state, of course, is the human state of heightened consciousness. As with athletes who operate from time to time in these altered states, psychics who search in this manner must be careful not to wander into traffic or step off cliffs. Often, they walk with an escort.

This is very similar to the Buddhist walking meditation where a group of people meditate while walking together in a cluster. Often, there will be a group leader to watch the meditators in this altered state. It helps to have someone else nearby to catch your fall if you falter.

Music of the Universe

One of my favorite practical uses of higher consciousness is personal enrichment. I like to listen to the music of the universe in this state. All of the great music ever composed, played, and hummed flows freely in the universe consciousness. Like all energized thought that has been released into the universe even unintentionally, the music never dies. This includes all the written and unwritten melodies of Mozart and the greatest performances of Franz Liszt and Billie Holliday. They continue to float in the collective conscious memory of the greater universe.

You can tap into this great reservoir of music, too. All you need to do is put yourself into a meditative state and enter heightened consciousness with the intent to hear music. This makes you a universal receiver. Of course, you can select specific kinds of music to inspire you, heal you, or cheer you up. Simply carry an image of the kind of music you intend you select. That will put you in the right place.

There is also a music of the universe that is seldom heard by anyone. Mystics have heard it. Musicians access it for inspiration. If Mozart wrote music that he heard inside his head like so much dictation, then he undoubtedly heard this rare and beautiful music of the universe. This music is not of this world. Except for the fragments that have been snatched from the universal consciousness and incorporated into music in our physical world, this uncommonly beautiful sound is beyond our world. It is impossible to even describe the instruments or voices that make this heavenly music.

This music can heal you and enrich your life. All you need to do is tune in the music and listen with your full awareness. This is far easier in higher consciousness than in normal consciousness, where the lower mind is so preoccupied and distracted by sensory overload from all directions. The higher mind is a listening mind, fully attentive. It lets the waves of sound roll over it and wash it clean. It allows itself to be purified and made whole. It brings this enrichment back to the physical body to be absorbed by every fiber of your being. This is the music of the soul.

Your soul instinctively loves music and craves music. And music feeds the soul, making it whole and fully alive. The awakened soul regenerates the body, making the body whole and fully alive. You need music to become a fully realized person.

The popular author Corinne Heline has written extensively about the esoteric aspect of many of the world's greatest composers. She suggests that the great composers all reached the fourth dimension for inspiration. The fourth dimension, of course, is beyond the physical dimensions of the ordinary world. One can reach beyond the ordinary world and its physical limitations, of course, through meditation.

Personally speaking, the most beautiful music I have ever heard were Pan pipes when I walked through woods in Oregon. I was in a state of heightened consciousness at the time. When I would begin to slip out of heightened consciousness, the divine music would begin to fade. The music was truly beautiful and beyond anything I have ever heard in the physical world during normal consciousness.

As with all meditation, it was hard to maintain heightened consciousness and hear the music the more physical I became in my walking. It is essential to shut down as much of the physical world as you can around you. I could not observe trees and hear music. I could not touch anything in my path and hear the music. I could not listen to the wind or the river. It was possible to perform a gentle walking meditation and hear this divine music, as long as I didn't become focused on too many aspects of the physical world around me. Do not allow yourself to become distracted. Enter higher consciousness with reverence and quiet. Give it your focused attention. There is much to be learned there.

Here is a meditation that might help you to hear this divine music of the universe.

Music of the Universe Exercise

You'll need:

- A quiet, isolated room
- A straight-back chair, or pad to lie upon, face up
- Dim lighting is best

Directions

1. Remove your shoes and loosen your clothes a bit, if you are not wearing loose-fitting garments.

2. Sit erect in the chair with feet firmly planted on the ground or lie face-up on the ground with hands at your sides or folded in your lap.

3. Close your eyes part way or altogether (whichever seems best to you).

4. Tune out all external distractions and cease all internal dialogue.

5. Allow the body to grow numb.

6. Shut down all sensory intake.

7. Allow the higher mind to take you into the higher consciousness.

8. Carry only one intention with you: *the desire to hear music in higher consciousness.*

9. Patiently wait to enter heightened awareness and hear the exotic and beautiful music of the universe. You must be very attentive. You must be very focused.

(Note: What did you hear? Can you remember any of it? If you did not hear music, be patient and practice this exercise again and again. It is very important that you completely surrender consciousness to the higher mind and shut down all sensory perceptions and lower mind functions of the body during this meditation exercise in order to achieve an out-of-body experience.)

CHAPTER 12

Some precautions

WE NEED TO include some final precautions here. There is nothing inherently dangerous or wrong with seizing the moment or practicing perceptive awareness, as described in the preceding chapters. The concern is that many self-improvement books give readers the false impression that a mastery of their newfound art can accomplish most anything for them at the expense of good common sense. Consequently, we need to discuss the practical use of time mastery through heightened awareness.

Even though you are limited only by your imagination in what you could achieve in a heightened state of consciousness and unrestricted by the physical laws of the universe, it's not always appropriate to enter this state. As with everything else in life, it's really a matter of timing. There are times when it is inappropriate. There are also limits as to what you should attempt, particularly in the beginning.

Obviously, entering into a meditative state or focusing your perception can be dangerous under the wrong situation. In the beginning of this book, I used the personal example of using perceptive awareness to avoid a car crash. I would hasten to add here that my options to avoid disaster in this situation were limited. I really needed to focus on an escape plan rather quickly. So I could take my attention off many other things in my immediate surroundings in order to focus. I knew that in the second or two before my possible crash, I could expect no other cars to approach me in this setting. I knew that no pedestrians were likely to jump in front of my car in the next second or two. My sense of smell wasn't needed to detect a fire or other telling odor in the next second or two. My hearing wasn't needed at that moment. Under all other driving conditions or while operating equipment of any sort, you normally need to stay alert with all of your five senses and stay in a normal state of consciousness. In such instances, you can't leave your body or focus your perceptive awareness. It's an obvious matter of safety and common sense. You can't mediate while driving a car. You can't enter a state of heightened consciousness while mowing the lawn, either. Don't even think about it.

Similarly, you should not attempt to enter a state of heightened consciousness while walking on a busy street or walking anywhere you could encounter traffic, dangerous obstacles, or ruts in the road. I used a personal example in the beginning of this book to describe my early encounters in sudden out-of-body experiences. I started walking down a busy, long street downtown in a conscious state, but then drifted into a subconscious state and continued walking in this fashion for a long distance. This could have been very dangerous. It was also very unsettling. Unfortunately, I had no control at that time and sort of drifted in and out of states of heightened consciousness with wild abandon. You will need to exercise control. Remember, you have will power. Remember, too, that your conscious mind is the gatekeeper. It decides when to open the gate to your subconscious mind and when to keep the gate closed. There is a wonderful Zen meditation where a group walks together in a meditative state. This is under a controlled setting. Don't wander through traffic in a meditative state.

The same cautions should be raised whenever you are caring for someone who needs your full attention or doing something that needs your full attention. You wouldn't want to let your body grow numb and enter into subconsciousness when you are holding a baby, for instance. Most day-to-day situations require your full attention and your conscious awareness with all five senses fully functional.

You wouldn't want to enter a state of heightened awareness when doing anything potentially dangerous, either, such as carrying a rifle or something you might not want to drop. Remember, the first step in perceptive awareness leading to heightened consciousness is to allow the body to go numb and focus your sensory awareness. That would mean temporary loss of the sense of touch. It might mean the temporary loss of your sense of balance. You really should be sitting down or lying down in a controlled, quiet setting in solitude to attempt a shift to this state of higher consciousness.

Moreover, you need to learn to control your entry into this state of higher consciousness and not just pop into it, as I described my early experiences. Believe me, it's quite frightening to return to your body after being out of your body in one of these experiences to find you've been walking down a busy street like some sort of semiconscious zombie! It's also unsettling to return to a state of normal consciousness to find you can't account for several minutes and worry what might have gone wrong while you sort of "left the room" unexpectedly. (I still regret the newspaper film I overexposed in the darkroom when I sat down during developing and then returned to my full senses long after that!)

You can avoid "popping into" a state of higher consciousness by keeping both feet firmly on the ground. Keep yourself grounded. Not unless you are full grounded in the here-and-now, with your full wits about you and all senses alert, should you even attempt to enter a state of higher consciousness. You must be aware of the fact that you sitting or reclining in a certain place and everything around you before you can safely allow your body to grow numb. Allow certain senses to shut down, still all sound around you and inside you, and enter a state of nonphysical reality. Consequently, you need to be in touch with your body and in touch with the physical world around you. Before you can become a master of time and space, first master your physical side.

Even if you practice caution in entering a state of heightened awareness under controlled conditions, you need to be aware that there is a limit to what you should expect to do. You should not just "pop in" on people unexpectedly in the physical world in an out-of-body state. If they see you or sense your presence in any way, it could be most unsettling to them. Really, it's an invasion of privacy. If you're visiting them to attempt to help them in some way, that's one thing. Just visiting for your own amusement is something else and selfishly rude. You might avoid this problem by informing such people of your plans to visit them, with their permission. If they are looking for you, they might even provide constructive feedback to you about the experience.

If you are attempting to help a sick friend through distance healing, astral healing, or thought forms, that's a noble use of heightened consciousness. We have seen in this book where many people claim success in energy healing in a heightened sense of awareness. Our thoughts are energy. We can project this energy. In case of illness, however, remember that energized healing should always act in tandem with application of traditional medical attention. Don't use energy healing as a substitute for traditional medical attention. If you are attempting to practice energy healing on yourself, always consult a medical professional in addition to your own efforts. There is no room for ego in the world of spirit. The spiritually evolved person is selfless and without the baggage of a huge personal ego. The sick need every bit of help they can get, including professional help. Your efforts to support them with your healing thoughts and your healing energy, however, can be very helpful.

Don't think that you are a superman or wonder woman, simply because you can enter a state of heightened awareness. You won't always be able to do incredible feats at a moment's notice, upon command. This is primarily because you will not always be able to access this state of higher consciousness. There will be situations that are so emotionally chaotic and disturbing that you will not be able to control your perceptive awareness to enter a state of higher consciousness. There are times of trouble that are so turbulent that your nerves will be pricked and all of your sense opened wide. In these situations, it will be difficult for you to allow your body to become calm, so that your bodily feelings are numbed and your perception is focused. At these moments, you are taking in everything around you in a frantic overload, all signals wide open and jammed open. It would be difficult for you to practice enough self-control to allow yourself to enter a state of heightened consciousness. That's where practice becomes important. Practice now, so you can enter this state of heightened consciousness when it's really needed, at a moment's notice.

Certainly, there are limits to what you might attain in this state of heightened consciousness, too. Sure, you can comb the legendary Akashik Records and explore worlds within worlds. But that won't necessarily help you balance your checkbook, establish a household budget, plan for your financial retirement, keep track of relatives' birthdays, or help you set and meet goals. Sometimes we have to remember to simply "chop wood and carry water" to get through some of the daily routine of living, to quote the title of a book by one Zen teacher. In the beginning of this book, I said how I would deviate from my daily planner whenever the time waves seemed right to do something else. In short, I suggested that we become opportunistic. I still think that's a good way to live your life. On the other hand, I wouldn't throw out the day planner altogether. There are times you really need to replenish groceries or take your car into the garage for scheduled maintenance. These things happen in the physical world, not in the astral world or a personal state of heightened consciousness.

Astral travel in a heightened state of awareness can be remarkable and take you to untold worlds within worlds. On the other hand, some worlds are best avoided. I can tell you about one level of the astral realm that I visited when I first started to have out-of-body experiences. It was a dense, orange world of hideous creatures. I could hardly move. I now realize that this place isn't the only level of the astral realm, but one level that I'd prefer to avoid in the future. You may encounter places you don't want to be when you begin exploring worlds through astral travel. Just be prepared to make a quick exit or find a helpful guide along the way. And if you encounter a proud and boastful deity presiding over a large sandbox, please don't tell him that I sent you. You're on your own now.

A Special Note to Readers

If you have experienced timelessness or instances where you "seized the moment" similar to the descriptions in this book, perhaps you would like to share your experiences for possible inclusion in a revised edition of this book.

The author welcomes your input. Please describe your personal experiences and send to:

Von Braschler
℅ Llewellyn Worldwide
P.O. Box 64383, Dept. 0-7387-0212-9
St. Paul, MN 55164-0383, U.S.A.

Thank You!

The author is donating half of all personal profits from the sale of this book to animal charities. *Thank you, readers, for making this possible!*

Bibliography

Abrams, David. *The Spell of the Sensuous.* New York, N.Y.: Pantheon Books, 1996.

Alcyone (J. Krishnamurti). *At the Feet of the Master.* Wheaton, Ill.: Theosophical Publishing House, 1970.

Arkani-Hamad, Nima, Sava Dimopoulous, and George Dvali, "The Universe's Unseen Dimension," *Scientific American,* August, 2000.

Besant, Annie. *Bhagavad Gita: The Lord's Song.* Adyar, India: Theosophical Publishing House.

———. *Thought Power.* Wheaton, Ill.: Theosophical Publishing House, 1988.

Besant, Annie, and C. W. Leadbeater. *Thought Forms.* Wheaton, Ill.: Theosophical Publishing House, 1997.

Blavatsky, Helena Petrovna. *The Voice of the Silence.* Wheaton, Ill.: Theosophical Publishing House, 1992.

———. *The Secret Doctrine.* Adyar, India: Theosophical Publishing House, 1979.

Bordow, Joan Wiener. *Swami Satchidananda: His Biography.* San Francisco, Calif.: Straight Arrow Books, 1970.

Carnie, L. V. *Chi Gung.* St. Paul, Minn.: Llewellyn Publications, 1999.

Castaneda, Carlos. *The Eagle's Gift.* New York, N.Y.: Pocket Books, 1991.

———. *Tales of Power.* New York, N.Y.: Pocket Books, 1991.

———. *A Separate Reality.* New York, N.Y.: Pocket Books, 1991.

Conway, D. J. *Flying without a Broom.* St. Paul, Minn.: Llewellyn Publications, 1995.

Dante, Alighieri. *Dante's The Divine Comedy.* New York, N.Y.: Chelsea House Publishers, 1987.

Fields, Rick. *Chop Wood, Carry Water.* Los Angeles, Calif.: Jeremy P. Tarcher, Inc., Putnam Publishing Group, 1984.

Gittner, Louis. *Listen, Listen, Listen.* Eastsound, Wash.: Touch the Heart Press, 1981.

———. *Love Is a Verb.* Eastsound, Wash.: Touch the Heart Press, 1987.

———. *There Is a Rainbow.* Eastsound, Wash.: Touch the Heart Press, 1981.

Heline, Corinne. *The Esoteric Music of Richard Wagner.* La Canada, Calif.: New Age Press, 1974.

Hewitt, William. *Self Hypnosis for a Better Life.* St. Paul, Minn.:Llewellyn Publications, 1997.

Johnson, Spencer. *Who Moved My Cheese?* New York, N.Y.: G. P. Putnam's Sons, Inc., 1998.

Jerome, John. *The Sweet Spot in Time.* New York, N.Y.: Touchstone, Simon & Schuster, Inc., 1980.

Karagulla, Shafica, and Dora Van Gelder Kunz. *The Chakras & the Human Energy Fields.* Wheaton, Ill.: Theosophical Publishing House, 1998.

Klemp, Harold. *The Dream Master.* Minneapolis, Minn.: Illuminated Way Publishing, Inc., 1993.

Krieger, Dolores. *The Therapeutic Touch: How to Use Your Hands to Help or to Heal.* New York, N.Y.: Prentice-Hall, Inc., 1979.

Krieger, Dolores, Erik Peper, and Sonia Ancoli. "Therapeutic Touch: Searching for Evidence of Physiological Change," *The Theosophical Research Journal,* December, 1986.

Krishnamurti, Jiddu. *Commentaries on Living.* Wheaton, Ill.: Theosophical Publishing House, 1995.

Kunz, Dora, and Erik Peper. "Fields and their Clinical Implications," *American Theosophist,* Nov. 1982, Jan. 1983, June 1983, Aug. 1984, Sept. 1984, and Nov. 1985 (six parts).

Leadbeater, Charles W. *The Chakras.* Wheaton, Ill.: Theosophical Publishing House, 1997.

Leek, Sybil. *Diary of a Witch.* Englewood Cliffs, N.J.: Prentice-Hall, 1968.

McLuhan, Marshall, and Quentin Fiore. *The Medium is the Message.* New York, N.Y.: Random House, 1967.

Merleau-Ponty, Maurice. *Phenomenology of Perception* (trans. By Colin Smith). London: Rutledge & Kegan, 1962.

Millman, Dan. *The Inner Athlete* (originally published as *The Warrior Athlete: Body, Mind and Spirit.*) Walpole, N.H.: Stillpoint Publishing, 1979.

Newton, Michael. *Journey of Souls.* St. Paul, Minn.: Llewellyn Publications, 1999.

Ouspensky, P. D. *Tertium Organum.* Kila, Mont.: Kessinger Publishing Company, 1998.

Paulson, Genevive Lewis. *Energy Focused Meditation*. St. Paul, Minn.: Llewellyn Publications, 2000.

———. *Kundalini and the Chakras*. St. Paul, Minn.: Llewellyn Publications, 1999.

Paulson, Genevive Lewis, and Stephen Paulson. *Reincarnation*. St. Paul, Minn.: Llewellyn Publications, 1997.

Pearce, Joseph Chilton. *The Crack in the Cosmic Egg*. New York, N.Y.: Julian Press, 1988.

Plato. *Complete Works by Plato*. Indianapolis, Ind.: Hackett Publishing Company, Incorporated, 1997.

Puharich, Andrija. *Uri: The Original and Authorized Biography of Uri Geller—The Man who Baffled Scientists*. London: W. H. Allen, 1974.

Roberts, Jane. *The Oversoul Seven Trilogy*. San Raphael, Calif.: Amber-Allen Publishing, 1995.

———. *Seth Speaks*. San Raphael, Calif.: Amber-Allen Publishing, 1995.

Skolimowski, Henryk. *The Theatre of the Mind*. Wheaton, Ill.: Theosophical Publishing House, 1984.

Smith, Ingram. *Truth Is a Pathless Land: A Journey with Krishnamurti*. Wheaton, Ill. Theosophical Publishing House, 1990.

Smith, Penelope. *Animals—Our Return to Wholeness*. Point Reyes, Calif.: Pegasus Publications, 1993.

Steiger, Brad. *Words from the Source*. Englewood Cliffs, N.J.: Prentice-Hall, Inc. 1975.

Twitchell, Paul. *Eckankar: The Key to Secret Worlds*. Menlo Park, Calif.: Illuminated Way Publishing, Inc., 1989.

———. *The Tiger's Fang*. Menlo Park, Calif.: Illuminated Way Press, 1967.

Vance, Bruce. *Dreamscape: Voyage in an Alternate Reality.* Wheaton, Ill.: Theosophical Publishing House, 1989.

———. *Mindscape: Exploring the Reality of Thought Forms.* Wheaton, Ill.: Theosophical Publishing House, 1990.

Vennells, David. *Reiki for Beginners.* St. Paul, Minn.: Llewellyn Publications, 1999.

Watts, Alan. *The Way of Zen.* New York, N.Y.: Pantheon, 1974.

Index

☾ REACH FOR THE MOON

Llewellyn publishes hundreds of books on your favorite subjects! To get these exciting books, including the ones on the following pages, check your local bookstore or order them directly from Llewellyn.

Order by Phone
- Call toll-free within the U.S. and Canada, 1-877-NEW-WRLD
- In Minnesota, call (651) 291-1970
- We accept VISA, MasterCard, and American Express

Order by Mail
- Send the full price of your order (MN residents add 7% sales tax)
  in U.S. funds, plus postage & handling to:
  Llewellyn Worldwide
  P.O. Box 64383, Dept. 0-7387-0212-9
  St. Paul, MN 55164–0383, U.S.A.

Postage & Handling
- **Standard** (U.S., Mexico, & Canada)

If your order is:

$20.00 or under, add $5.00

$20.01–$100.00, add $6.00

Over $100, shipping is free

(Continental U.S. orders ship UPS. AK, HI, PR, & P.O. Boxes ship USPS 1st class. Mex. & Can. ship PMB.)

- **Second Day Air** (Continental U.S. only): $10.00 for one book + $1.00 per each additional book
- **Express** (AK, HI, & PR only) [Not available for P.O. Box delivery. For street address delivery only.]: $15.00 for one book + $1.00 per each additional book
- **International Surface Mail:** Add $1.00 per item
- **International Airmail:** Books—Add the retail price of each item; Non-book items—Add $5.00 per item

Please allow 4–6 weeks for delivery on all orders.
Postage and handling rates subject to change.

Discounts
We offer a 20% discount to group leaders or agents. You must order a minimum of 5 copies of the same book to get our special quantity price.

Free Catalog
Get a free copy of our color catalog, *New Worlds of Mind and Spirit*. Subscribe for just $10.00 in the United States and Canada ($30.00 overseas, airmail). Call 1-877-NEW-WRLD today!

Visit our website at www.llewellyn.com for more information.

Mind Magic
Techniques for
Transforming Your Life

Marta Hiatt, Ph.D.

Access the incredible, unused power of your mind

Create a life of greater abundance, love, health, and inner peace with life-transforming techniques that really expand your consciousness. There is no power in the world as great as the forces residing in your own mind, and self-hypnosis is a direct pipeline whereby you can release these powers.

A definite, strong idea, when held constantly in the mind, can change the biochemistry of the brain so it will no longer be programmed to failure. Part I of *Mind Magic* explains the nature of consciousness and how the mind works. Part II is a practical handbook on how to apply the theory, with chapters on self-hypnosis, affirmations to attract love and financial success, self-healing techniques, and guided visualizations.

For the skeptic, this book provides a comprehensive understanding of the scientific basis for new-age thinking. For the devout, it will provide a thoughtful spiritual base for transformation.

- Learn why the techniques of guided visualization and hypnosis actually work
- Expand your consciousness, increase your happiness, improve your financial situation, let love really work in your life, and transform your ideas of limitation
- Reprogram your mind to eliminate negative ideas so that you may live happily and prosperously

1-56718-339-5, 264 pp., 6 x 9, illus.   **$12.95**

Reiki for Beginners
Mastering Natural Healing Techniques

David Vennells

Reiki is a simple yet profound system of hands-on healing developed in Japan during the 1800s. Millions of people worldwide have already benefited from its peaceful healing intelligence that transcends cultural and religious boundaries. It can have a profound effect on health and well-being by re-balancing, cleansing, and renewing your internal energy system.

Reiki for Beginners gives you the very basic and practical principles of using Reiki as a simple healing technique, as well as its more deeply spiritual aspects as a tool for personal growth and self-awareness. Unravel your inner mysteries, heal your wounds, and discover your potential for great happiness. Follow the history of Reiki, from founder Dr. Mikao Usui's search for a universal healing technique, to the current development of a global Reiki community. Also included are many new ideas, techniques, advice, philosophies, contemplations, and meditations that you can use to deepen and enhance your practice.

1-56718-767-6, 264 pp., 5 ³⁄₁₆ x 8, illus.   **$12.95**

Also available in Spanish

To order by phone, call 1-877-NEW WRLD
Prices subject to change without notice

Chakras for Beginners
A Guide to Balancing Your Chakra Energies

David Pond

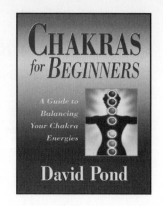

The chakras are spinning vortexes of energy located just in front of your spine and positioned from the tailbone to the crown of the head. They are a map of your inner world—your relationship to yourself and how you experience energy. They are also the batteries for the various levels of your life energy. The freedom with which energy can flow back and forth between you and the universe correlates directly to your total health and well-being.

Blocks or restrictions in this energy flow expresses itself as disease, discomfort, lack of energy, fear, or an emotional imbalance. By acquainting yourself with the chakra system, how they work and how they should operate optimally, you can perceive your own blocks and restrictions and develop guidelines for relieving entanglements.

The chakras stand out as the most useful model for you to identify how your energy is expressing itself. With *Chakras for Beginners* you will discover what is causing any imbalances, how to bring your energies back into alignment, and how to achieve higher levels of consciousness.

1-56718-537-1, 216 pp., 5 ³/₁₆ x 8   **$9.95**

Also available in Spanish

To order by phone, call 1-877-NEW WRLD
Prices subject to change without notice